DYING TO SUCCEED

Phillip James Walls Jr.

Dying to Succeed
© 2020 by Phillip Walls

ISBN (Print): 978-0-99875-192-4
ISBN (eBook): 978-0-99875-193-1

TABLE OF CONTENTS

DEDICATIONS

The one constant in my life has been my lovely, understanding wife. She has stood with me every step of the way with the utmost encouragement and support. We have been on a long, tumultuous journey together, and we have managed to come out on the other side changed but not defeated. We have weathered one storm after the other as God has directed us through each and every one. I would have had a very difficult time completing this journey without her help and support, and I truly dedicate the completion of this work to her. I love my wife dearly, and I am so thankful that God put her by my side. She has been more to me than I could have ever imagined.

DYING TO SUCCEED

INTRODUCTION

Have you ever wondered why so many people become successful after a near-death experience or life-changing event? After all, they are the same person they were before these traumatic incidents, and yet, something in them awakened the instant they were revived.

The moment they realize that nothing gets completed in death, a sense of urgency drapes over them. Once they have had a brush with death, the life that they are now living just doesn't seem to make sense. They open their eyes and notice that they are not where they are supposed to be. No more disingenuous assessments or false narratives created through hopes and dreams of a life not yet lived.

Many of them see themselves living the life that they want to live when, in reality, they are living a life far below their own expectations. Fantasy is much more powerful than reality. Most people choose to live more in the imaginary world to escape their truth. Many feel that they deserve more and that they can and will do better. However, they spend too much time chasing their fantasies rather than doing the things that's necessary to make their dreams come true.

All of their lives they search for what they believe will make them happy. Society has shown them what happiness is supposed to look like. Higher education, a great paying job with a Fortune 500 company, a luxury car, two-and-half kids and a beautiful house in the suburbs—once they have all these things, society has led them to believe that they should be totally happy. Right?

What if there was a formula that anyone could adopt that would give them everything they needed to completely create the exact life that they wanted? What if these methods have already been proven? Every tool that's needed for success in life is in this book. This is not a book giving people just enough to set them up for volume II. Nor is this book a revamped version of other familiar books out there on the market today. This is a book that stays with you for a lifetime, a book that you go back to over and over again until the principles are a part of who you are.

There are detailed examples for every area of your life. After perusing this material, you will quickly begin to realize that you have not lived life to your fullest potential. You have not done enough or helped enough or made as much as you should have. You have not made a significant difference as you had expected. Nevertheless, you know that you don't like where you are, and the near-death experience snaps you right back to your reality.

As life flashes before your eyes, you do not see the end that you thought you would, so now something has to actively be done.

When you strongly feel like you have been given a second chance, now it is time to get dead serious about how to get the things you want. Everything that's been done to this point has not worked, which means that you have to do something out of the ordinary.

A sense of urgency overcomes you, and one revelation after the other surfaces, giving you a strong indication that many things in you have to die. The old philosophies must die, ineffective habits must die, everything you believed about being successful must die, but more importantly, the lackadaisical effort about how to get the things you want must die.

This tool will help elevate you to a higher level, and you will experience a life change. Many things are buried in death, and sometimes in death, life flourishes. Out in the wild, one animal dies so that another thrives. It is an ongoing cycle in the animal kingdom. The same holds true for you. There must be a continuous cycle of things dying inside so other things can flourish and grow. There are ideologies, viewpoints, influences and habits inside of you that must die so that you can become what you were designed to be. The things you consistently do every day will shape who you become.

Most people are saturated with negative thoughts, incidents and feelings from childhood to adulthood. You have no clue how much damage has been done until you begin the painstaking process of in-depth evaluation about what's not working and why.

Once you can figure out what's hindering you, there is a freedom to allow those parts of you to die. Why, metaphorically, must you die once the things that are not working have been identified?

Death is a key part of life, and this is a continuous cycle no matter who you are. You bury the dead, understanding that you will never see their physical body again nor hear their voice, smell their perfume or cologne nor experience their gentle words of encouragement.

As painful as it is, whatever you discover that's not working not only must die, but be buried as to never return into your consciousness again. How do you do that? What formula can you use to remove years of negative data? You must replace the old way with the new. You are reborn, so to speak, and your new self is on a mission. Everything that you were can never ever return.

Once you are impregnated with a new idea, the death of the old life is imminent. You become consumed with a sense of purpose to begin and complete all the things you never got started. It then becomes very clear where you stand in relation to your current position in life. The hard, cold fact is that the life you imagined never became a realization because of something that you did or didn't do. This is the very moment that you recognize your condition and summon every ounce of who you have become to die.

This book will help you through the techniques necessary for lasting life change. The old paradigm will be gone never to return or be regurgitated. Everything in this book was written to transform you into exactly what it is that you want to be.

You begin this very instant to renew your mind and recreate yourselves into that dynamic person God made you to be. The life you are living was all created by something or someone other than yourself, and you can no longer hide from the shell of a person that society has molded you into.

Mechanisms designed to keep you in the status quo are no longer effective, and the baggage carried for so long suddenly has no hold on you. You see someone different in the mirror. You see a person that's always been there but was buried in a deep sea of propaganda for the purpose of adhering to the needs of the wealthy. Now that you see the real and capable you, there is nothing on earth that will stop you from achieving anything that you decide to do.

CHAPTER ONE

All That You Are Must Die

In order to make dramatic change in life, one must first die to self. The Bible says in the book of John Chapter 12 Verse 24, "Truly, truly, I say to you, unless a grain of wheat falls into the earth and dies, it remains alone; but if it dies, it bears much fruit." Death allows us to make the necessary paradigm shifts that bring about lasting change. All our lives, we have been subjected to an outpouring of negativity. Limitation funneled into us by our surroundings and those close to us. The reality is that most of the world around us is negative, and we are subjected to those influences while in that environment.

Many of us have absolutely no clue what we have been inundated with especially during the ages between one and five years old when our subconscious minds are wide open and in a 100 percent receptive state. As children, we don't even develop a consciousness until around age six or seven. Our conscious mind acts as a protection mechanism regarding what we let into our subjective mind. It is the guard at the palace. It decides what comes in and what goes out. The subjective mind is the inner mind or subconscious mind. Once we are able to decide what to think and how to think, it is oftentimes too late. We have already been exposed to whatever environment our parents had us in. The thing is that our parents could only pass on to us the level of knowledge and wisdom that they had.

When we take a long hard look at our lives and decide to ask ourselves some serious questions such as, "Am I living the life that I want to live?" If not, why not? Pretty basic question, right? Yet, many of us will never ask this question, because even if we ask, what do we really know about who we are if most of our lives were shaped at a very early age? Other questions to consider are, "Are my aspirations, desires, attachments, perceptions and behavior truly of my own creation?" "Am I being authentic with myself and those around me?" "Am I pursuing those things in life that I choose, or am I living out an idea rooted in my mind by someone else?" "Am I allowing myself to develop enough to function at my fullest potential by accepting change and welcoming challenges?" "Have you ever attempted to make a dramatic change in your life for the better, but regardless of how many positive affirmations you read or how much visualization you did, you ended up right back in the same old place of lack and destitution? Why would that be?" Undoubtedly, there has been no paradigm shift in your life, so the results continue to be what they have always been. A complete paradigm shift has to happen in order to get permanent and lasting outcomes.

We must literally die to self to become what it is that we desire to be. The Bible says, "Call those things that be not as though they were." So how do we do that? First, we must be willing to roll up our sleeves and do the work. Removing years of negative impressions on a young mind will take a lot of effort, persistence and consistency to reprogram. Remember, it literally took years to pour all this mess into us, and it will take some time to plant new seeds. Once these new seeds are planted, they must be allowed the due process of growth. The new thoughts that have now been planted in your mind by our very nature will attract like thoughts. The process of change inevitably begins. The changes that need to be made for lasting results will not happen unless we are willing to completely die in every aspect imaginable. If we want to truly be free, we must die to old beliefs. We must die to what we think we know about success. We must die to our assumptions about what it takes to become successful. Everything that has gotten us to this point must all die. Why? Because nothing that we really want in life has materialized, and it's all because of the paradigm that we are now living in. Change the paradigm; change the results. It's that simple. Our current paradigm has not worked, and it won't, because it is terribly flawed. If it wasn't, we would have everything we desired, and since we don't, we must begin with the obvious. We must create a brand-new paradigm. Easier said than done, right?

Well, first, we must have a burning desire to change who we are. The very first step to any type of change begins with a deep, inner, honest evaluation of who we really are and what action steps we need to take each day to change our programming. Self-evaluation is a very difficult thing to do because facing the truth about how we were raised or what kind of environment we came out of can be very disappointing. Yet, we must face and overcome that feeling of disappointment.

Once we have identified how we became who we are, it is imperative that we now take accountability for what we must do going forward to change into who we want to become. A plan must be generated and action steps created. Finding out who we are and how we got there is only part of the change process. Now we must develop a plan of action that will move us in the right direction. Learn to do what is necessary to redesign what someone else created in you.

Fear, like anything else, can be eliminated. Identifying it and then doing what we fear and the death of fear is certain. The more we do this, the easier it becomes to completely master the emotion of fear. Nothing is more powerful than knowing that fear no longer has control of our lives. Many of us harbor different fears. Some have a fear of swimming, talking in front of audiences, skydiving and zip lining or para-sailing. Some have a fear of in-depth examination because of what they might find. Until we honestly find out who we are and how we got to be who we are, it is literally impossible to make a permanent change.

Transformation usually begins by first taking a look at those things that are working in our lives. No matter what situation we find ourselves in, there is good stuff happening. When we are thankful for the blessings in our lives, we have a starting point to begin building a positive foundation. Concentrating on the good things prevents us from tearing ourselves down before going through the process of in-depth evaluation. Honest self-assessment is a very difficult process, because recognizing what is keeping us in a certain state takes complete truthfulness and a whole lot of accountability. Seeing ourselves as being responsible for what we have created is a scenario we don't want to accept, and yet, no one else made the decisions that got us where we are today.

We ultimately made every single decision that put us in the situations we find ourselves in. We chose not to attend college because of disinterest or unwillingness, and now we are dissatisfied with our income. We chose not to take a promotion offered to us because it was more responsibility than we wanted to deal with. We started dating the first person that showed interest in us because we were tired of being alone. You moved into the house that you're living in because rents were too high across town. The choices go on and on. You look outside yourself, at others, to seek the reasons behind these choices: because no one helped you enough, or cared enough, or told you enough. Now the harsh reality is that, no matter what you believe about your circumstance, you and only you created it. If your parents didn't have the knowledge to teach you, it's not their fault. They could only pass on whatever knowledge was rooted in them.

Even if your parents and those involved in your upbringing filled your mind with views and perceptions that they thought would benefit you but did not, they were still doing all they knew to do at the time. Our parents worked with the views, ideologies and perceptions that were passed on to them, and the only thing they knew to do was pass those on to you, whether they were helpful or destructive.

Once you become an adult, it is up to you to exert yourself to become what it is that you want to become. Take accountability for your past, present and future decisions, and then your mind will shift and begin processing this new change. Once your mind has accepted responsibility for who you have become by owning up to these past, present and future decisions, it will start looking for ways to help transform you into the new image you have presented. Without a doubt, in a short while, the old you will no longer exist and your journey in life will take a different turn. The fork in the road regarding decisions won't be as challenging or fearful. The paradigm shift will produce very different outcomes than what you are accustomed to, as you seem to be getting luckier and luckier with each choice. Once you understand how crucial it is to simply take accountability, you'll begin to grow in confidence and your entire demeanor will be much different than the one characterized in your old paradigm.

There is no longer a need to carry all of the resentment, anger or blaming of someone or something outside yourself. The level of understanding about recognizing internal vulnerabilities that have kept us stuck has now provided a vehicle for continual self-evaluation and the promotion of ongoing growth. Have you ever noticed that, no matter what happens in some people's lives, they seem to handle any issue with ease? Then have you been around people who seem to have problems handling even the smallest of issues? They can have the exact same problems but completely different views about how to handle them. What's the reason? One chooses to take accountability for how they are going to respond to unexpected events, while the other does not. There are only two choices about how you are going to respond to anything.

You will either find a positive approach or a negative one, and the one that you habitually do is the one you will always lean towards. We condition ourselves to react a certain way about the issues we are confronted with. Once the habit has been formulated, our reaction will either produce a lack of stress or a great deal of stress. When we don't handle stress well, we suffer from a lot of negative emotions such as depression, anger, envy, resentment, hopelessness and even jealousy.

We tend to find ourselves feeling overwhelmed with the slightest unplanned event. This eventually causes all other types of issues down the line that make our lives even more uncomfortable, like illness or life-threatening diseases. On the other hand, there are those who go through life and it appears to be smooth sailing. Not much at all seems to affect them or their attitude. These people understand that, in life, things happen unexpectedly. Cars break down, air conditioners stop working, microwaves quit and people sometimes get sick, because life happens whether we want it to or not. The only thing we can control is how we are going to approach any particular problem.

Are we going to address our issues with a solution-oriented mindset or a woe-is-me mindset? Are we asking ourselves how I can resolve this issue or what's possible now, as opposed to why me or how could this happen? Every issue that comes our way gives us an opportunity to grow into a possibility thinker rather than a woe-is-me believer. Possibility-thinking shifts your mind into a different gear. It's in what I call "seeking mode." When your mind is in seeking mode, it is reaching far beyond your mental capacity to solve problems.

The Bible says in 1 Corinthians 2:10-11, "But God hath revealed *them* unto us by his Spirit: for the Spirit searcheth all things, yea, the deep things of God. For what man knoweth the things of a man, save the spirit of man which is in him? Even so the things of God knoweth no man, but the Spirit of God." According to this verse, there should be nothing that we are not able to solve or find the answer to. Our Spirit Man is able to search out the deep things of God, and God has answers for every situation.

The philosophies of this world system have no place in the spiritual realm and will offer us no comfort. There are no answers in a system designed to keep us stuck, maneuvering our every turn in life through mazes of doubt, confusion, deception and false hopes. Everything inbred in us by this system must die so that we can live the life that Jesus died on the cross for—a full, happy, abundant life without fear, stress or worry.

We have been conditioned to believe that status is more important than doing what's right. Our desire to have more has overtaken our sense of compassion, degraded others self-worth and blinded our eyes to God's way of doing things.

Dying to self is a process garnered with mixed emotions. When we look at ourselves in the mirror and ask the right questions, we no longer continue to kid ourselves about how we got in the situation that we are in. We begin to clearly see how our entire life unfolded and the how and the why of every major decision that has gotten us exactly where we are right now.

The conditioning process began the instant you pushed your way through the birth canal and sprung out of your mother's womb. There waiting for you were two loving parents full of what the worldview had already created in them to pass right along to you. They were excited to bring you into the world, and made plans to teach you everything they could about how to be healthy, happy and successful. Whatever system your parents have adhered to is totally out of your control. If God is the head of their life and His wisdom is guiding and teaching them, then you have a chance of developing in a Kingdom system, which is God's system. Then there is the world system or the Babylonian system.

The Kingdom system is a monarchy. In this system, God is the final authority. His government down here on earth is structured by ordained pastors, elders, deacons, evangelist, prophets, apostles and teachers. Jesus came down from Heaven to establish God's government. He chose the apostles to set up and teach those ordained how the churches were to be governed. God's government has specific rules within the church that all Kingdom citizens abide by. These rules are clearly outlined in the Bible. A pastor is the head of the church. His role is to oversee and teach the flock. His guidance comes from the power and gifting of the Holy Spirit. This is a far different approach from the world system.

The Babylonian system is very precise and methodical. It's a bureaucracy. The people are governed by heads of state, and each of them have different ideas and philosophies about how to govern. From the time you learn to walk, talk and read, you are highly persuaded to follow along the same maze of life that many before have travelled. Realistically, we were set up to be molded into the next worker bee for huge manufacturers, large businesses, hospitals and corporate law firms. There will be many out there offended by this statement, but because something is not popular to say, it doesn't mean it is any less veritable. Most of us have heard this recording: grow up, go to school, get good grades, go to college get a degree and get a good job so you can work for a good company and retire in thirty years.

In today's corporate structure, this is very rarely even a possibility. Many are lucky to get five years, let alone thirty. Business philosophy has changed. Most companies are not interested in keeping someone around for thirty years anymore. We can't rely on the traditional belief that this matters today. It does not.

The Babylonian system charms you into believing that happiness and success lie in producing huge outcomes for someone else to enjoy. Thoughts are very rarely interjected into our minds about entrepreneurship, inventions or creative careers that offer self-reliance or independence from this world system. The world system preys on the worker bees, which are the middle to upper-middle class. The few at the top (the one percenters) earn most of the wealth, while the rest battle for what's left over and, at the same time, fuel the economy. The middle to upper-middle class are as critical to the world economy as worker bees are to the hive.

According to an article written by Pew Research Center, the middle class accounts for around 51 percent of the US population. This is why the bulk of the financial burden lies on their shoulders. When we wake up and realize what has been done and why, it is clear why this system collapses every few years in the form of recessions.

From the time we are born, this world system is pounded into us from all directions. It first starts with our parents and our loved ones. Everything they have soaked up during their lifetime by way of family, friends, work associates, social media and news outlets is passed directly on to us. Once we become of age, we are deluged with a constant barrage of fake news, untruths and misdirection to satisfy an insatiable desire to obtain wealth and power.

Everything that society has shaped us to become must die. We have been programmed to serve by design. The idea of happiness and success has been tenuously projected on the screens of our minds since birth, and like any well-oiled machine, it has worked to perfection. Many of us walk around in a hypnotic daze truly believing that we created who we have become without ever realizing that we became exactly what the world system expected.

This is why self-examination must occur if we ever plan to receive revelation about what happened to us and why. From these revelations, we can decide to unlearn everything bad that the world system has instilled in us, and begin to reprogram our own minds to perform the greatness that God has placed in us. In order to rebuild something new, we must tear down what's old. The illusion that we have been walking around in took years of well-planned orchestrated events that appealed to our five senses of taste, touch, smell, hearing and seeing. To reprogram our minds in a matter of months as opposed to years, our approach has to be unorthodox. It has to be something uncomfortable to the status quo. It has to go beyond the five senses, into a much deeper realm.

One of the quickest methods of imprinting images upon the inner mind is visualization. Whenever we use our creative resources to bring about those things that we have dreamed, the manifestation comes quicker and is certain. God says in Deuteronomy Chapter 6 Verses 6–9, "And these words, which I command thee this day, shall be in thine heart: And thou shalt teach them diligently unto thy children, and shalt talk of them when thou sittest in thine house, and when thou walkest by the way, and when thou liest down, and when thou risest up. And thou shalt bind them for a sign upon thine hand, and they shall be as frontlets between thine eyes. And thou shalt write them upon the posts of thy house, and on thy gates."

Everything begins with a thought. That thought becomes an idea, and that idea becomes a vision. God is telling us here that, in order to get things deep down in our heart, we must talk about it all day long. Talk about it when we are sitting in our house, when we are walking in the park or down the street, before we lay our heads down to sleep and when we rise up in the mornings. On top of all that, he said to write it on the posts of our house and on the gates. What we talk about all day long is what we become. The words we speak have power. They create the very world that we live in. Yet, we clearly have difficulty changing what we say. How many times have you heard someone say something like, "This headache is killing me" or "I am sick and tired of getting up going to work"? What about "If he does that one more time, I'm going to shoot myself in the head" or how about "My feet are just killing me"?

Are these things really killing you, or is this some expression that you have heard from someone else? Whatever the reason, it doesn't matter, because these words are creating exactly what you say. Whatever you have spoken has already been created, and sooner or later it will manifest itself. One way to start the process of dying to self is by focusing on what we are saying day in and day out. If we are speaking things that we did not create, then we are speaking what someone else has created in us. There is no way that we would vocalize such destructive statements as "Oh stop it; you're killing me" or "Man my head hurts so bad I just want to cut it off." Someone passed those words on to us, and we adopted them with open arms. But when we get somewhere quiet, all alone and in a dark place, our spirit starts opening our eyes and our minds to the truth.

We begin to clearly see that we have been strategically developed to fit into a system designed for just a few to really enjoy. This Babylonian system is not God's system. This system is based on capitalism. Sowing and reaping is and always will be God's system. It works perfectly in every aspect of our lives. Whether it be the thoughts we think, the words we speak or the things we do, this system works as God designed. We definitely reap what we sow.

Have you ever taken the time to listen to what most folks are saying and then look at their lives? What you mostly find is that they are receiving what they have been speaking. If they have been speaking poverty, you will see poverty in their lives. If they have been speaking fear, you will notice that they are fearful. If they speak against others all the time, those very things operate against them. God is not mocked. We reap what we sow in every single area of our lives. It is not just what we materially give in the way of money or goods, but also by words and actions.

Ever heard that, for every action, there is an equal and opposite reaction? This is Newton's Third Law of Motion. When you throw a punch, the very same force that's generated moving forward is also being generated in the opposite direction. That is where power is created from a punch. This is also where the Law of Polarity comes into effect. Everything has an opposite. If there is a positive, there is a negative. If there is darkness, there must be light. Where there is love, there is hate. Where there is joy, there is sadness. It does not matter what it is spiritually or materially, everything has an opposite. Now think about the words we choose. There are only two choices when speaking about anything: positive and negative. Since we have a choice every single time we speak, why not choose the positive regardless of what your situation looks like, because what it looks like and what it is are two entirely different things.

There are facts that can really have you feeling gloom and discouragement. It can seem that things are not looking so great, and staying focused on the facts can lead you to a place of fear, uncertainty and despair. Facts and truth may look and feel similar, but they are very different. The fact is that the doctors have diagnosed you with cancer. The fact is that your flesh may not feel so good. The truth is, by His stripes you are healed. The truth is that death and life are in the power of the tongue. The truth is that you can call those things that be not as though they were. To be different than what facts are telling you is to think different than what facts actually are.

The old way of thinking must die. You must adapt to a new view of yourself. Like anything, adaptation takes a deep embedded desire to change. Summon the power that's in you to do what you have to so that you can actually do the things that you want to. There is no secret. There is no magic wand. There are no genies. God is not going to snap His fingers and, bam, everything you want appears before you. There are no carpet rides, and self-pity won't bring in a new horizon. At some point, you have to relegate in your mind that God has provided you all that you need to achieve whatever it is that you set your mind to do. Notice the word "set." It's a verb, and as we all know, verbs do something. Action moves things in motion, and motion is what makes things happen. Don't let your hands be idle or let your mind be molded to a deceptive worldview of who you should be. Rise up, and take your crown. Own what you have become so that you can change it and decide right now to be what it is that you have imagined.

Die to the instincts of flesh and bone, and live by the innate power of the Holy Spirit. It will guide you to every right opportunity and lead you down pathways of honor and prestige. We must always keep in mind that we are spirit clothed in flesh. It is our spirit that commands the body and not the body that controls the spirit. Our spirit knows what is right and good, because it was created by God. The spirit is our Heavenly compass. It will always guide us in the same direction as God. It gives us the spiritual insight to any problem.

Think about what it actually means to die to self. It means to die to flesh and the things that the flesh desires. When we are operating in the fleshly realm and not the spiritual, then we succumb to fleshly desires. Our emotions take control of most everything we do. We make decisions on the basis of how we feel. We react on the basis of some emotion. Whether it is the emotion of fear, anger, worry, doubt or love, our emotions can cloud our thinking and swallow us up with feelings of insecurity and confusion. We have trouble making decisions, and we can sometimes fail to recognize the walls that have been established over our lifetimes.

The world has designed a system that churns day and night like clockwork. It has been strategically produced over time to create a never-ending supply of human capital necessary to maintain this multi-trillion-dollar world economy. God's economy is a very different type of economy. It is designed for those with plenty to turn a compassionate eye to those starving and in need. The world economy is a system built on fleshly traits such as fear, greed, poverty and insecurity. Those who have plenty are in fear of losing what they have, and regardless of how much they have accumulated, fear of losing it all keeps many from living a truly joyful life: the more you have, the more others try to get it from you. One of the easiest routes to wealth for many is to find a way to rob, steal, con or extort money from those who have accumulated it.

People who think this way don't see enough value in themselves to achieve this kind of life. Instead, they spend their time scheming and planning to take what someone else has earned. Your wealth does not lie in someone else's backyard; it resides in you. But your failure to recognize your value leaves you stuck believing that your only option is to seek it some other way even if it's illegal or immoral.

Every person, place or thing that is prevalent in your life right now was placed there to help you get to your destiny. Even those that are in doubt of your capabilities or those who speak against where you are going are there to strengthen you on your journey. Do not get caught up in what others are saying or believing about what you are trying to accomplish. Just know that they have their purpose, and you may not know until you have reached your destination what their purpose really was—or you may never know. Never concern yourself with what someone else's role is or isn't in your life. Just flow with the natural law of life and let them do what they do on your behalf, but stay focused on the end result. Once your true purpose has been identified, your subconscious mind will find ways to help you formulate habits necessary to effectively operate in your purpose.

No one or anything on earth can stop you from achieving whatever you have set your mind to do. Pitfalls, obstacles and failures are an expected part of the journey, and realizing that before you start will prepare you to keep going in spite of these events. Winners win because they are fully prepared to win. They accept that there will be good days and bad days, and they are equally valued as they progress towards their higher purpose.

How we see ourselves is what determines how our lives will be structured. You will elevate to the level of your thinking. Why is it that some earn billions of dollars over their lifetime, while others barely meet the poverty line? Their internal value systems are very different. One carries an internal value system of overflow and abundance that is never-ending, while others carry an internal system of lack and destitution. Now many may believe that some don't have a choice. They were born in an impoverished household where despair was just an everyday part of life and it was their normal. Based on their normal, they have been ingrained with a mindset that is irreversible.

Then there are those who are born privileged. They have been sent to the best schools that money can buy. They have been inundated with the idea of wealth and abundance all their lives, and are bound to continue in that trend. None of this is true, and none of it matters. Regardless of what hand you were dealt in life, you still have the option to undo whatever damage has been done in your younger years.

At some point, you must release what others have done with good intent, and come to terms with the reality of personal accountability. No matter what your parents taught you, instilled in you or surrendered to, once you become responsible for your own means, the same holds true for what's housed in your own mind.

There comes a time when blaming outside influences or other affiliations about the life you own no longer bears any relevance. You must decide to conscientiously scrutinize everything you've been taught and why. Often, you will find that everyone who poured into your life had the best intentions with little to no knowledge of the effect of their teachings.

People can only pour into you what they were influenced by; therefore, if you were molded to accept their views, perceptions and insights, then you are only a reflection of those who invested in you. This is why it is absolutely imperative to know who influenced your life so that you can see who you are based on where you came from.

If you can evaluate with an open mind who was responsible for your development, most likely, the same flaws and ideologies that you see in them are the same ones that probably exist in you. This is your starting point of beginning to die to self.

Evaluation of any kind has no merit if the information is not used to transform from what you are to what you want to be. Saying the right words at the right time around the right people will not bring about change. You must have the utmost integrity about what has been discovered, and instead of hiding from it or placing it on a shelf to deal with later, resolve in your mind that this is a very serious matter. Understand that things in you must die so that you can experience a rebirth of new paradigms and unlimited possibilities. Reshape your mind so that you can shape your world from this day on. Be the captain of your ship.

Reshaping your life for the purpose of recognizing and achieving your destiny takes a tremendous amount of determination and focus along with the ability to overcome obstacles. Making room for setbacks and unexpected events during your journey will not only prevent discouragement, but help you create a realistic, doable timeline for its attainment.

It is also a good idea to start with the end in mind and work your way backwards. See the project finished in its entirety. Envision it in your mind. See yourself getting rave reviews and all the accolades that come along with the completion of a successful project. Now make plans to get to that end result that you see in your mind. Then make up your mind to see it through no matter what.

Get in the habit of finishing what you start. Develop a winning attitude, and see yourself always winning. You'll be amazed at the outcomes and the things that you will accomplish. Never see yourself failing, only succeeding. Set your own mind up for success, and you will succeed. This is no one else's journey, so you don't have to seek others' opinions about what you are doing. Just get about the business of making it a reality.

People around you are usually quick to offer their opinion about what it is that you are doing as well as their criticisms. Don't ever listen to the views and comments of those who are observing you but aren't doing anything of any significance themselves. If you need advice, seek it from those who have done what you are doing or who are themselves successful.

Go after your vision with an expectation that you will achieve it. Expectation works in tandem with belief. When they are working together, your desire is heightened and focus is magnified to help ensure that your mind and activities stay set on the task at hand.

Belief is created by repetitive thoughts. A thought comes into your mind, and that thought brings you joy and happiness. The thought lines up with what is inside of you. Because the thought triggers an influx of like thoughts, you begin to develop a burning desire. That burning desire eventually turns into belief. Once you believe, you are on your way to accomplishing the very thing that you are striving for.

Believing is the key component to ignite your imagination, which is where many of your answers will come from to help you along your journey. Creation lives in the imagination. For many, imagination lies dormant from a lack of use. It will never go away because it is a part of our design; therefore, it can be awakened anytime we choose. Of course, it will take painstaking effort to reignite, but it is doable. Once the imagination becomes engaged in the process of finishing your project, you will develop a confident expectation.

Expectation is developed by the level of your faith. If you have little faith, you will most likely have low expectations. If you have great faith, you will have high expectations. You will only receive in life what you expect. Let's say there are two people that graduate college at the same time with the same degrees and with the same experience. One has expectation to land a good job making $50,000 to $60,000 annually. The other has an expectation to earn $100,000 a year. They each will search and apply for work on the basis of their expectations. Your expectations will guide you towards the level of income that you believe you deserve. It will not lead you to anything greater than your own expectations. So, expectations are a key component to living a different lifestyle.

Now let's get back to the two college graduates. Straight out of college, neither of them may make the money they have envisioned, but they both will eventually work up to their expectations. The one with the lower expectations will take promotions and positions that gets him to the level of $60,000, while the one who has the higher expectations of earning $100,000 will pursue opportunities and ways to get to what they expect.

If your goal in life is to be a millionaire, then you must have faith, confidence and expectations to become a millionaire. Why not have huge expectations? Whether you think big or small, it takes the exact same amount of energy, so why not think big?

God is the source of our supply, and our God is a big God. He is more than willing and capable of giving you whatever it is that you expect.

If God turns the entire ocean to liquid gold, and He tells you to go to that ocean of gold and grab the amount of gold according to your expectations, why would you bring a teaspoon when you could bring a semi-truck? Others will bring a thousand semi-trucks. After all, God gave no limit. He said to get as much as the level of your expectation.

Life is no different. It will only give what you expect out of it. Of course, just because you expect it, doesn't mean that it will fall into your lap with little to no effort. There will be failed timelines, unexpected setbacks, unplanned interruptions and dependence on others that you can't control. But just remember that we have victories on the other side of our failures and possibilities beyond our pain. You will overcome these struggles.

This is one of the main reasons for in-depth, honest self-assessment before beginning your journey. It will prepare you for unexpected events and unplanned situations without ever getting discouraged to the point of quitting.

Decide before you begin your journey that quitting is not an option. You are working from the end of your vision backwards, so you have already seen its completion; therefore, everything in between now and the end are all just stepping stones towards an awesome future.

CHAPTER TWO

Reflection is Part of the Metamorphosis

Blatant honesty about who you are is the only way to recognize what must die. Deep down, many of us know who we are, and being totally honest with ourselves is a very difficult task. When we are completely forthright, we really start getting the understanding that our life is not exactly what we designed it to be.

If you always do what you've always done, you'll always get what you've always got. No matter how gruesome, pitiful or dreadful it is, we created it by our thoughts and the words we have spoken. Some have never realized the magnitude of a spoken word. Remember, God spoke the Heaven and earth into existence, and He gave us the same power. It doesn't matter whether we realize what He has given us or not; it still works the same way for both good and bad.

No one has to tell you that the sun will rise tomorrow—you already know that it will. Whether you're in a dark pit or a cave, whether you are in a position to see or not see, it doesn't matter. The sun is going to rise. Gravity doesn't have to be defended because it works regardless of who uses it. If a billionaire jumps off of a twenty-story building, they will most likely be a dead billionaire. If a homeless person did the same thing, then guess what? They would be a dead homeless person, because gravity will do its job without question.

The same thing happens with our spoken words. Once they are spoken and go forth, they will create something. So, the first thing when dealing with metamorphosis is understanding that change happens and transition must come. We don't have to do anything at all, and change is happening. Every day that you wake up, you are a day older. Every seven years, every cell in your body has been rebuilt without your ever having to lift a finger. So change occurs without our permission. If change happens no matter what, then why not have some control of those changes by speaking the life we want to live, the health we want to have, the money we want to earn or the vision we want to send forth that will eventually become our legacy?

The reality you are living is not the reality of your vision; it is the reality you have created on the basis of the thoughts you have allowed. We can write our story any way that we want simply by changing what we think, say and do. If the metamorphosis process begins with a shift in our thinking, then a change must come in the words that we speak and, lastly, we must develop the belief system that lines up with what we say. So, three things must change: our thoughts, our words and our beliefs.

How do we change a thought about who we are or what we deserve? One of the best ways is to read everything that you can get your hands on. Read God's word as often as possible. Read books on positive thinking, self-help books, literature on paradigm shifts, and writings about how to create wealth. Read everything available that will transform your thinking and your concepts to those that will attract more of what you want and none of the things that you don't want. Read authors like Ernest Holmes (*Science of the Mind*), Napoleon Hill (*Think and Grow Rich*), John Maxwell (*The 15 Invaluable Laws of Growth*) and Dr. Bill Winston (*The Law of Confession*). These are great books to have in your arsenal for self-development and growth. This kind of reading will help change how you think and what you say.

Go buy some three-by-five index cards, and write on them things you want ingrained in your mind. For example, on one of the cards I read several times a day, I wrote, "I am so happy and grateful now that money comes to me in increasing quantities through multiple sources on a continuous basis." Where did I pick this phrase up from, and how did it become important to me? I was listening to a Bob Proctor video on YouTube about changing your paradigm, and in that video, he mentioned and talked about the significance of this one phrase and how it dramatically changed his life and income.

So another avenue to help us adapt a different perspective are videos. Not just any videos. Listen to people who have become a great success spiritually and financially, and listen to what they did and what resources they used. For instance, I listen to or read guys like John Maxwell, Earl Shoaff, Bob Proctor, Earl Nightingale, Napoleon Hill, Tony Robbins, Les Brown, Ernest Holmes and Eric Thomas. Of course, there are many more, but these people have been around for some time teaching others how to transform into what they want to become.

Sometimes I read various index cards with positive affirmations on them fifty to hundred times a day until they are memorized. I read statements that I have created just for me, and I read them first thing in the morning and at night right before falling off to sleep. I want the part of my mind that represents 95 percent of my brain to be at work while I am sleeping, so I make a diligent effort to read and imagine right before I doze off. The more I began to believe it, the more my life began to change for the better.

At times, we have unexpectedly received checks in the mail, or we've had people bless us with a check and, all of a sudden, money just started rolling in from every direction, and all I had to do was read some writing written on a three-by-five index card. Of course, I also had to believe what I was reading every day for it to manifest.

You see, when God spoke things into existence, He had absolutely no doubt about whether it was going to happen or not. He expected those things that He spoke to manifest. He has endowed us, His creation, with the exact same ability. It is our faith about what we say that brings them into our lives. Faith that you will or faith that you won't all work the same way. Say what you mean, and mean what you say. The thoughts that you think followed by the words that you speak aligned with your level of belief will change your way of thinking. Ever heard the saying that talk is cheap or that action speaks louder than words?

Can you imagine how Muhammad Ali's career would have turned out had he not backed up what he said? He professed to be the greatest of all time, and his belief in himself and his capabilities propelled him into being a sports legend. He has been called the greatest athlete of our century. Was it by accident? Absolutely not. He did exactly what he expected himself to do, and that was to become a world heavyweight champion like no other before him nor anyone after him. What was so remarkable is that he became world heavyweight champion three different times against three different opponents. According to odds, he was not expected to win a single one of those fights, and yet, he shook up the world. How was it possible for Ali to do what he did? It all started with what he was saying to himself about himself.

He publicly declared to be the greatest every opportunity he had. He convinced himself that he was a champion before he ever defeated any of those opponents in the ring. When he took on the mindset of a champion, he did everything necessary to become exactly what he proclaimed himself to be.

He walked and talked like a champion. He trained like a champion, and he ate and lived like a champion. He would get up every morning at 5:30 a.m. He would loosen up by doing some stretching exercises. He would then go on a six-mile run to improve stamina. After he ran, he would eat a hearty breakfast of all-natural foods along with orange juice and water. He would head over to the gym by 12:30 p.m. and start warm-ups with some stretching and dancing around on his toes practicing movement and balance. He would then do five three-minute sessions of shadow-boxing with thirty-second rest periods in between. He would do six three-minute sessions hitting the heavy bag. Next, he would do his sparring session with a sparring partner. From there, he did nine minutes on the speed bag, twenty minutes on the jump rope and one minute of shadow-boxing. Then he would do sit-ups on an inversion table with legs straight up and down. Next was a session of sit-ups with slightly bent knees. From sit-ups, he would move to the bicycle crunch and from there more jump roping side to side and back and forth. He would end the day with a full body massage, and then head home. Dinner would consist of chicken, steak, green beans, potatoes, fruits, fruit juice and water.

This was the training regimen of a champion. It never mattered how he felt, he trained the same way every single day. Everything you say and believe matters.

The next step to changing your paradigm is to find some influential friends who are positive and enthusiastic and are elevated in their thinking. They will pour into your life if you will let them. If it is wisdom you seek, then first ask of God who gives liberally. Then find someone who walks in wisdom, and spend time with them. If it is money you are after, find a millionaire or two or three to treat to lunch, and just sit there and listen.

Learn from those who already have what you are looking for. Whether it's someone you personally know or a video or even books, but find someone or something that you emulate. Once you have befriended or associated yourself with those that will help grow you, regardless of how much they already have, treat them. Buy their lunch or dinner. What you will receive in knowledge and education from the time spent with them will far outweigh the cost of the lunch or dinner.

You must think outside your normal way of doing things in order to reap the benefit of growing into what you want to become. These kinds of activities will most certainly begin to shift your thinking. Once your thoughts change, the words that come out of your mouth will be very different than before. You will begin to speak with more confidence. Your conversations will be riddled with enthusiasm. You will begin to speak those things that you want as if you already have them. You will begin to understand that you are a creator and the life you want already exists inside of you. Whatever you really believe and have faith in is what will manifest in your life.

Don't rely on others to help you achieve your dreams. Don't relinquish your purpose to appease those who don't understand your journey. Leave behind those things that have not served you, and stay focused on those things that will grow you. This is your dream, so take ownership until it is realized. God will send those necessary to help fulfill your dream; however, you are still accountable for producing the action steps necessary to achieve it. All the resources you need will be provided to you with little to no effort on your part. If your God-given talent is that of public speaking, but you need a speech writer, then God will send you someone to write speeches. If you are a mathematical genius, but scheduling an itinerary is not your strong suit, a scheduler will be brought into your life.

Moses stuttered and, yet, God chose him to lead His people out of bondage. God sent him a speaker without relinquishing his responsibility. Moses was still the chosen leader by God and was still held accountable in spite of his perceived deficiency. Not having all of the necessary tools or skills are never reasons to not pursue your dream. There are always others who have all that you need and will be made available to you at exactly the right time. When you have really taken the necessary time to honestly evaluate who you are and what God has placed in you, a true picture of your capabilities begins to come to light. At this juncture, you begin to delve deeper into the whys and how's of transformation. Your mind acknowledges that your journey has just begun, as your metamorphosis continues and all of the roughness of life is spewed out and your determination has shown you a clear path to success. Like the butterfly, we experience four key stages in the metamorphosis process.

First, we identify and recognize the condition of a diseased mindset and the effect it has had on our lives up until now. Second, we take the time to create a plan that institutes a new direction. Third, goals are constructed that match the dreams that we have laid out for ourselves, and lastly, the dream is fulfilled. All of this takes dogged belief. Every thought you possess, seeking real change, has to first be believed without question. We all have heard the saying "What the mind can conceive and believe, it can achieve." This boils down to one word—faith.

The Bible clearly states that we must walk by faith and not by sight. Faith is simply a deep belief that what you envision is as real as if it had already happened. Your mind's eye is the vision that God has placed in you, and your faith will pull that vision from the invisible world to the material world without any doubt. If you have the aptitude within you to imagine a thing, or have the focus to think about it consistently, by design it will be delivered to you.

The world around us is like a very large warehouse, and this warehouse has everything in it that you could possibly imagine. It is all at your disposal to pick and choose as you please. All you have to do is imagine and believe. Faith moves mountains. Every goal, dream or desire will be realized as long as you really believe. Don't let fear disrupt or kill your vision, because, with certainty, it will. Don't stay stuck on your failures. They are simply stepping stones towards an amazing future. Don't allow stumbling blocks and pitfalls to rob you of your dreams. Spend time preparing your mind to receive what you have envisioned for your future.

When God gives you a snapshot of who you are to become, there are no anomalies. Everything is perfect and in order. Nothing is distorted or out of place. Everything in your vision is precisely as it should be, and this is exactly how it will be manifested. Realizing that your visions are an extrapolation of what's to come will cause you to exert a deeper evaluation of what's needed for its materialization. It will motivate you to gauge every single thought, emotion, habit and philosophy that's been adapted over time. Your subconscious mind will begin to find ways to supplant old values and beliefs and start interjecting new traits and ideas that will move you towards your destiny. Our thoughts are used to ignite actions drawn from the subconscious mind to bring into reality the movie that's been played over and over in our mind's eye.

The life that you have imagined began with a single thought. Once we think a thing that we truly believe is accessible, then all of the energy sources within us begin to formulate ways to transform them into the material. Many construe a thought to be an idea, and an idea is a conception of something not yet realized. It is birthed in the mind, and as the idea is repeated over and over, a burning desire begins to bubble up within. Once this desire becomes encapsulated with belief, actions will be produced to move you towards your desire. In the book entitled *Think and Grow Rich* by Napoleon Hill, he gives several examples of the power of thought. He begins with the story of a young man by the name of Edwin C. Barnes (pages 24–25).

It all began when he stepped out of a freight train in a place called Orange, New Jersey. He had the appearance of a tramp, but his thoughts were those of a king! He imagined himself standing in Edison's presence. He could picture himself asking Mr. Edison for an opportunity to carry out the one consuming obsession of his life—a burning desire to become a business associate of the great inventor.

Barnes' desire was not a hope! It was not a wish! It was a keen, pulsating desire that transcended everything else. It was definite. The desire was not new when he approached Edison. It had been Barnes' dominating desire for a long time. In the beginning, when the desire first appeared in his mind, it may have been—probably was—only a wish, but it was no mere wish when he appeared before Edison with it.

A few years later, Edwin C. Barnes again stood before Edison, in the same office where he first met the inventor. This time, his desire had been translated into reality. He was in business with Edison. The dominating dream of his life had become a reality.

Edwin C. Barnes began his journey of becoming a business associate of the great inventor Thomas Edison with a single thought. This thought became a burning desire, and he became obsessed with the idea of partnering with Edison. Even though Barnes had the appearance of an ordinary street bum, he was glowing with confidence. He had a definiteness of purpose, which was to work alongside the great Thomas Edison. He burst into Mr. Edison's laboratory and boldly announced that he had come to form a partnership with him. All those who worked alongside Edison were in disbelief and ridiculed young Edwin C. Barnes. Thomas Edison did not join in but, instead, saw a young man determined to do what was necessary to help bring his vision into reality. Edison was fascinated with his aspiration, and decided to give him an opportunity as a floor sweeper. Thought will generate in you an overpowering ability to direct all your focus towards the thing that it has set its sights on.

Many people who have left an indelible mark on society began with a dream. Henry Ford had no money and very little education, and yet, he imagined people riding around in horseless carriages. He started right where he was with what he had. He did not wait for opportunity to come knocking. He created it. He left home at the age of sixteen to take an apprenticeship as a machinist for a ship building company in Detroit. After some time, he became very skillful at operating and servicing steam engines. In 1890, Ford was hired on at the Detroit Edison Company as an engineer. He still had a strong desire to design and build the first horseless carriage, and in 1893, he built his first gasoline-operated buggy. Ford continued learning and educating himself through various failed attempts at building cars and businesses, and finally in 1903, the Ford Motor Company was birthed. Now Ford Motor Company is a household name, and the evidence of his tenacity to pursue his dream is evident all over the world.

Thomas Edison dreamed of a lamp that could be operated by electricity. He began where he stood to put his dream into action, and despite more than a thousand failures, he stood by that dream until he made it a physical reality. Thomas Edison gave society some of the greatest inventions known to mankind. He invented the phonograph, the movie camera, the carbon microphone, the quadruplex telegraph and much more. But his most extraordinary invention by far was the incandescent light bulb. This one invention transformed our world as we know it today. We went from candlelight to coal oil lamps to incandescent light bulbs to the magnificent world of modern lighting that we now experience. Practical dreamers do not quit.

Martin Luther King had a thought that evolved and became a dream. On August 28, 1963, that dream was launched and shared with an entire nation. That dream was poured into the hearts and minds of every man, woman and child listening that day and beyond. It was a dream of such great magnitude that it has been cultivated and intertwined throughout society since its inception. That one dream from the mind of one man still lives in us today and still continues to impact us.

I can still feel the power of the very first sentence. "I have a dream that one day this nation will rise up and live out the true meaning of its creed: 'We hold these truths to be self-evident, that all men are created equal.'" I was but a child living in a small town in a Jim-Crow-riddled South. Tears flowed down my face, and my life has never been the same.

Lincoln dreamed of freedom for the slaves with little to no support, put his plan into action and accomplished one of the world-changing events historically recorded. Because of this great accomplishment, Lincoln is regarded as one of our greatest presidents. A thought that all men and women should be treated with dignity and respect and the ownership of human beings was just plain wrong ignited a nation into a civil war. It was probably one of the most difficult decisions of his presidency, and yet, the United States looks very different today because of it.

The Wright brothers dreamed of a machine that would fly through the air. A helicopter-like toy that their father gave them as children planted a seed. That seed bloomed into an idea that men could indeed travel one day in a flying machine. Now, we travel all over the world on something called an airplane—a thought that became an idea, which soon after became a reality. The first notion of this idea drew overwhelming criticism and a barrage of ridicule, but the Wright brothers would not stop until their dream became a reality (pages 29–30).

Anyone who has dramatically changed the world had to do some very deep reflection and self-evaluation. These great men and women could not have endured all of the negative feedback, ridicule and lack of support without first knowing who they were and what they carried inside them. They were driven by something greater than their reputations, or other people's viewpoints. They were far beyond the epitomes of failure and defeat. They had seen everything necessary to push themselves forward at all costs. They were operating from a clear and present vision. They knew what the end result looked like, because they had already been there countless times in their minds.

This kind of discipline and focus only comes through in-depth self-reflection and dire understanding of who you are. Once you have determined who you are, you start addressing any and all roadblocks. You begin to boldly confront mental obstructions poured into you during your lifetime. Things you used to be apprehensive about no longer carry the same effect. Doubt and worry begin to fall off as you become more aware of what it takes to get to the finish line. Now you have been made aware that what you discovered during this in-depth evaluation has existed all along, and the false narratives that you allowed to sink into your mind were never a part of your true design.

You were created in the image of God, and He passed on to you the same characteristics that He himself possesses. Every word that we speak has huge significance regarding what we bring into our lives. Our words have far more power than we realize. God's design is a perfect design and operates with great precision. He did not give us the spirit of fear but of love and of power and of a sound mind.

Since God gave us a sound mind, He gave the ability to truthfully assess ourselves mentally and emotionally. We know ourselves better than anyone. We know every thought we think whether good or bad or indifferent. We clearly understand why we don't like certain things and why we love others. We are better in tune with our own emotions than any doctor or psychiatrist. We either keep quiet about what we know so that we don't reveal to anyone else how we really think, or we won't give the real reasons for emotional breakdown and destructive outburst.

We have this same problem when it comes to our own selves. We look in the mirror and deny the truth about what we see in that mirror, which is one of the reasons we have difficulty in transforming from who we are into who we want to be.

The challenges of getting exactly what we want in life has never been someone or something outside ourselves. It has always been the inability to be honest with the person in the mirror.

Most of the decisions that we fail to make are all normally centered on some type of fear. We create so many excuses not to act on what we know to be true. We fear making the wrong decision. We know what we see in the mirror, but it is too painful to acknowledge that we have failed our own selves. We fear what others may think or not think. We are clearly focused on all the wrong things. We must at some point learn to address and face fear as opposed to letting fear quell our Kingdom purpose. We must concentrate on getting fear out of the way at all costs.

CHAPTER THREE

Get Fear out of the Way

F ear will always keep you in a state of deficiency. Fear paralyzes you into non-action, and that will keep you poor. One of the basic laws of the universe is the law of vibration. This law stipulates that everything is in motion and constantly moving. When you speak a word, your voice has a certain vibration or movement, and that does one of two things: it brings things to you or moves things away from you depending on what you say and how you say it

For instance, if I say, "I feel great and everything always goes my way." Guess what? You will most likely feel great, and things will somehow always go your way. Why? Because you have set in motion that very thing at a vibrational level. On the other hand, you could also say, "I feel lousy today and nothing ever seems to go right for me." Well, you will feel lousy, and things will never go as planned.

Notice that one statement is bringing things to you, and the other is moving things away from you. Fear acts as a repellant. It strips us of our freedom: our freedom to imagine, our freedom to explore new possibilities and our freedom to be creative. Fear derails hopes and dreams. It shatters everything in its line of sight without thought or regard for consequences. It prevents good things from happening in your life, because fear pushes while confidence attracts.

Fear is normally displaying a lack of confidence or a lack of knowledge; either way, it keeps you in a state of deficiency. So many who live in fear act as though they are powerless and have no recourse. They play the victim. Those who are socially oppressed say, "No one understands. I am always being attacked or belittled. No one gives me a break. I am afraid of pursuing my dreams because I will be judged or rejected."

Then there are those who self-impose an atmosphere of failure. "If I go after my dreams, I might fail. I don't have the skills necessary to be successful." One debilitating thought after the other—fear is nothing but a mental collection of small thinking and poor programming.

Unless we are being chased by a wild grizzly bear to be devoured or falling off of a cliff facing imminent death, fear is just a lifetime of destructive self-talk of garbage in and garbage out. It is difficult for most of us to face or discuss fear, because the truth is that most of us are running from ourselves rather than any actual danger.

According to Napoleon Hill, author of *Think and Grow Rich*, there are six basic fears that keep us locked into the life we are living. Most of us are strongly affected by one of the first three fears: fear of poverty, fear of criticism and fear of poor health. The remaining fears are fear of loss, whether it be someone you love or the death of a loved one, fear of getting old and fear of death. This is probably the longest chapter in the book, and because fear chokes the life out of most dreams, I want to really discuss all six components. The fear of being poor is probably the most detrimental of the six.

Poverty and riches can't exist in the same mind. The main reason is that poverty and riches constitute totally opposite spectrums. If you truly desire wealth, you must resolve in your mind that any circumstance leading towards poverty cannot be accepted. Obtaining riches has to begin with a true evaluation of your core belief system and how it was adapted. The desire to change your entire mindset about wealth has to be the primary emotion that engages you to act. Why did I choose the word engage? Because the word engage means to pursue, follow up on, act on, go after, quest for, operate and employ. These are all action words, and no real change in life happens without putting in an enormous amount of work.

Now I am not talking about physical, laborious efforts like shoveling dirt or digging ditches. The real work has to be done psychologically. You have to be prepared to make a complete shift in your thinking. Whatever you have set in your mind to receive is exactly what you will get. Impoverished thinking draws poverty into your life; whereas a wealthy mindset will reward you with riches. It is like anything worth achieving: you must first see yourself in that state to create a strong desire. This is what will incite action steps and attract resources to get you moving towards what you are seeking. Make no mistake here; desire is the key component necessary to obtain riches. It is the driver that makes the impossible possible.

Next is a clear-cut plan on how you are going to create wealth. What price are you willing to pay to achieve what it is that you desire? What amount of money will it take to satisfy all your financial needs? Like anyone taking a long journey or sailing across the ocean, you must know what the path is to get there. Regardless of how tedious or frustrating this step seems to you, knowing how to get there will be a key part of your success.

Sit down and develop a road map to your new destiny. Write down on paper exactly how much money you want to earn and what skill sets you have or will need to accomplish your goal. Determine what resources are currently available to you. Don't look for ways to lose. Learn to only focus on those things that will help you win. Change your associates, move to a better environment, read books and find value in people. You will never achieve anything great in your life without finding a way to service people. It doesn't matter what service you choose; as long as it is done with excellence, wealth is attainable. Do whatever is necessary to train yourself to overcome fear.

Fear of being poor is a state of mind. This mental state will ruin any chances of elevating your life in any area. During the Great

Depression, fear ran rampant as many lost huge fortunes overnight. Panicking investors caused the stock market to crash by unloading over 16 million shares of stock on October 24, 1929. Fear destroys all sense of reason. It immobilizes creativity, it obliterates enthusiasm, it affects self-control and, most importantly, it prevents us from identifying our purpose. Fear can strip desire, cause uncertainty, cause a loss of focus and eliminate ambition. Knowing why we exist and what we should be doing is what keeps us motivated beyond catastrophes. It helps us move around road blocks and unforeseen problems with laser-like focus and determination. Fear causes a life of unhappiness and magnifies self-doubt. Out of all six, fear of poverty is the most harmful.

Overcoming fear is not an easy task. It takes a lot of intentional activities to alleviate this beast called fear. Willingness to be truthful about the things you fear is a very valuable step in the process of change. Realizing those fears is still not enough; they must be accepted and then dealt with. Until the outright pain and humiliation of poverty has been experienced, it is very difficult to muster up enough drive to change this condition.

Reflection of life regarding self and position will help you identify your strengths and weaknesses. Deep honest analysis will reveal not only what's not working, but also what traits already exist that will help transform an impoverished mindset into that of higher self-worth and increased income. Without going through this painstaking evaluation of self, there can be no expectation of opening up creative channels that will bring abundance and prosperity. If this is something that you are unable to do, inquire of those who are close to you who will give an honest assessment of your capabilities and areas that need improvement.

Dramatic change is not for the weak at heart, which is why only 1 percent of the population lives a life that many only dream of—a life of opulence that provides every indulgence known to man with unflinching concern for how much it costs.

Have you ever observed a person who has no job, no home, no income and no hope? Their whole demeanor tells a story of lack and despair. Their shoulders droop, and their eyes reflect the shame and humiliation of being poor; they project a loss of hope. They have fallen to the bottom of a disgraceful, unforgiving pit of defeat while constantly being belted with a barrage of failed opportunities. Poverty breeds poverty. Those living in poverty have conditioned themselves to accept living in poverty; therefore, overcoming a life of poverty will never materialize.

Why do I have this insight about poverty? Because I have been there. I have curled up in small crevices near buildings in attempts to shelter myself from the wind and rain. I have gone days without eating, not by choice, but because I had no food and no money and no job. I have wandered from park to park in hopes of finding a spot that I could call my own. That never happened, because other homeless persons out there were looking for the exact same thing.

I felt that society had dumped me into this quagmire of despair to test my mettle, to see if I would survive. Like so many before me, survival was my primary goal in life for a very long time. But there becomes a point that something inside you gets tired of blaming everyone and everything on the outside. There is a time that you realize everything you need exists within you and that nothing from the outside is going to change what's on the inside. I had to decide that being homeless was not an option. I had to decide to have the basic dignity of eating a meal every day, having a roof over my head and clothes on my back. I had to acknowledge how I got to this place and accept responsibility for putting myself there.

At times, you must sacrifice the company of those who hinder you to make room for those who will help propel you to greatness. Being alone without food, shelter, warmth and companionship is by far one of the most destructive states that I have ever experienced. I would never have changed my condition if I had not taken full responsibility for my circumstance. I had to recondition my mind to accept loneliness in order to conquer limiting beliefs. It was at that point in my life that I came to the realization that I could create a different scenario. I could come out of my situation by truly understanding how I got there. Up until that moment, I had been exposed only to poverty and everything that came with it. When you live in constant poverty, your whole life is a life of inadequacy. There is always a shortage: not enough money to pay bills, buy food, provide clothing or enjoy basic entertainment like a movie or dinner at a restaurant.

You see yourself as less valuable and feel ostracized just because of your financial position. The expression of "I can't afford that or this" becomes an everyday staple in your life, because inadequacy is what you have become accustomed to. You feel emotionally drained because there is never enough of anything, especially money. You wake up the next day to repeat the same old things the same old way because you really believe that this is your life and you have no clue how to change it. You want to change it, and you struggle to understand why you are not. You find yourself running the same old program day after day, month after month, year after year because your paradigm has not changed.

Oddly enough, you don't even take the time to evaluate how to get out of what you are in. You don't think past the problem, because you are living in the problem. When your mind is geared to think in terms of shortage, it is not in the mode of being solution oriented. It is not searching for answers. It is just looking for a way to survive the next shortage. People around you that are not in the situation don't understand why you can't turn things around. Some of the thoughts and philosophies about money and finances were poured into you during your early years.

The paradigm that you are walking around with is not of your own creation. Whoever you are was created at a very early age; probably at five or six you had already been shaped and conditioned for the rest of your life.

"From the time of conception until the first day of kindergarten, development proceeds at a pace exceeding that of any subsequent stage of life. Efforts to understand this process have revealed the myriad and remarkable accomplishments of the early childhood period, as well as the serious problems that confront some young children and their families long before school entry. A fundamental paradox exists and is unavoidable: development in the early years is both highly robust and highly vulnerable. Our conclusion is unequivocal; what happens during the first months and years matters a lot, not because this period of development provides an indelible blueprint for adult well- being, but because it sets either a sturdy or fragile stage for what follows."

—Jack P. Shonkoff and Deborah A. Phillips

Earlier I had mentioned that poverty breeds poverty. Why would that be a true statement? Because during a child's first five to six years of life, everything that they hear or are exposed to is implanted into their subconscious mind. They have no mechanism in place to avert or reject negative information or less-than-favorable environments. If a child is born into poverty and is not exposed to anything else, they will develop an impoverished mindset, and this will be ingrained in them without their having any idea. They will become adults not knowing why they continue to struggle financially.

"From birth to age 5, children rapidly develop foundational capabilities on which subsequent development builds. In addition to their remarkable linguistic and cognitive gains, they exhibit dramatic progress in their emotional, social, regulatory and moral capacities. All of these critical dimensions of early development are intertwined and each requires focused attention."

—Jack P. Shonkoff and Deborah A. Phillips

Some of the methods used for changing a person's paradigm are reading, associations or change of environment. Unless a person gets a revelation, poverty will be a perpetual cycle regardless of what attempt is made to create a life of wealth. You are stuck in a life that someone else created and passed on to you.

Potential exists in every human being, and yet, to realize it, you must be able to develop a clear path through the muck of poverty etched in your mind. There is nothing exciting about living in a constant state of lack and deprivation. Like anything, there is always hope for change, but in order to realize that hope, you must first recognize that there is something in you that needs to see beyond the poverty instilled in you.

Many of those in your circle will harshly judge your decision to eliminate fear in your life. That's okay, because most are speaking to you from their own place of fear. What they are really telling you is that they are afraid to attempt the thing you are doing because they can't see themselves doing it.

There is an analogy of a jar full of crabs. One crab will be persistent about getting to the top of the jar and jumping out to a place of freedom, but when that crab is at the very top of the jar, one below it will pull it down back inside the jar with the rest. Many humans are very much the same way in that it is much easier to derail your dream and keep you at their level than it is for them to see you succeed. If you make it out of the jar, what about them? They can't see themselves climbing out of the jar, so they stay.

If the effort is too great to fulfill your dream, then you have not yet found the dream that ignites your desire. In John Maxwell's book *The Fifteen Invaluable Laws of Growth*, he states, "The price of anything is the amount of life you are willing to exchange for it." When you want something that you've never had, you must do something you've never done to get it; otherwise, you keep getting the same results (page 179).

Have you ever wondered why you keep circling around to the same old spot? You find yourself struggling with money, or time, or relationships, or keeping employment, and it seems to always be someone or something else outside yourself causing these problems. Well, the only common denominator is you. Every situation that we find ourselves in is most likely caused by some decision that we made or didn't make. The sooner we take responsibility for our mess, the sooner we can get ourselves out of the mess.

Paradigm shifts take time, persistence and a strong will to change. The less time you have been exposed to negative influences, the easier it will be to make a mental change. The longer you have been exposed to negativity and poor choices, the more effort it will take to make a shift in your thinking. Depending on what you were exposed to in your early years, professional intervention may be required to help you recognize what was passed on to you and why.

"Parents and other regular caregivers in children's
lives are 'active ingredients' of environmental influence

during the early childhood period. Children grow and thrive in the context of close and dependable relationships that provide love and nurturance, security, responsive interaction and encouragement for exploration. Without at least one such relationship, development is disrupted and the consequences can be severe and long- lasting.

Children's early development depends on the health and well-being of their parents. Yet, the daily experiences of a significant number of young children are burdened by untreated mental health problems in our families, recurrent exposure to family violence, and the psychological fallout from living in a demoralized and violent neighborhood. Circumstances characterized by multiple, interrelated and cumulative risk impose particularly heavy developmental burdens during early childhood and are most likely to incur substantial costs to both the individual and society in the future."

—Jack P. Shonkoff and Deborah A. Phillips

Knowing where you came from and how those in your life during your early years impacted your philosophies, perceptions and character not only helps you better understand where and how a lot of your fears and inhibitions were developed, but now gives you the necessary information and understanding of what needs to be removed. Most often, people who believe that they are criticizing you are really criticizing what someone else has placed in you. Which brings to mind the next component of fear.

Fear of criticism is a stumbling block that hinders success. Many are looking for acceptance from someone else: a parent, a spouse, a brother or sister or even a close friend or relative. In any case, looking outside of yourself for approval doesn't mean that you will avoid criticism. In fact, the further you move away from their level of thinking, the more you will be criticized. Does this mean that you are moving in the wrong direction? Actually, you are propelling yourself down a path that many cannot and will not follow.

The Bible says that we will reap what we sow. Part of that reaping is stripping away bad influences and unfruitful relationships to make room for those that will elevate and help improve your life. People who hold on to impoverished mindsets cannot see down the same road that you are travelling because they have been in a limited, conditioned space for so long that they are unable to expand their horizons.

There is a very popular story of what happens when you place a pumpkin the size of a walnut inside of a small jar. The pumpkin can never grow any larger than the size of that small jar. Sometimes in order to expand, you must change your environment. Some people never move to a bigger jar. Moving to the unfamiliar is terrifying, but for just a little while, because eventually, you will expand to the size of your new environment. You will never realize your dream until you grow to the size of your dream. Stretching beyond the limit of one's belief is not something that most are accustomed to. If you have *big* dreams, you will be investing a lot of time on self-improvement to expand to the size of your dream. Many will be lost along the way, because they will not dare go where you're going and you can't wait for them to catch up without forfeiting your dream.

Don't risk your success by keeping bad company. Understand that criticism represents a deep fear of losing someone or being left behind. In either case, old relationships will drop off and new ones will be developed the closer you get to your destiny. Most everyone you meet will tell you that they want to be successful and, yet, if you were to ask the question "What are you doing to achieve success?" many will have no answer nor a plan to get there.

Whenever you're seeking to achieve something life-changing, wishing for it will not bring it to fruition. Having others pray it into existence for you will not make it real. Hanging out with those who have already achieved what you want in life will not produce it for you. There will be benefits to your being involved with those who already have what you want, and that is education. However, education alone is still not enough. There must be a strong desire to make a change, and then a sensible and realistic plan along with action steps will move you towards your dream.

A writer can never write a book without first sitting down and putting ink to paper. Hanging around other writers is not going to get their book written for them. They must empty their thoughts to tell their story, and the only way to do that is to write. Does it need to make sense when you first start? No. Just getting your inner thoughts written down is the main action step. From that, a story begins to unfold, and before you know it, a book has been created for all to enjoy or learn from.

The habit of action will always move you towards what you are seeking, whereas inaction will stagnate or pull you away. Failure is a fact of life. People fail and they fail and they fail, but each failure is a stepping stone to success and gives you a better understanding of how not to do it the next time. I am amazed at how easily some are pulled away from their dreams. One failure or one mishap puts them in quitting mode.

A quitter never wins, and a winner never quits. Giving up, like anything else, is a habitual act and not part of our design. I memorized the poem below, and every time I thought about quitting, I would recite this poem.

Don't Quit

When things go wrong as they sometimes will,

When the road you're trudging seems all up hill,

When the funds are low and the debts are high,

And you want to smile, but you have to sigh,

When care is pressing you down a bit,

Rest if you must, but don't you quit.

Life is queer with its twists and turns

As every one of us sometimes learns

And many of failures turns about

When they might have won had they stuck it out;

Don't give up though the pace seems slow—

You may succeed with another blow.

Success is failure turned inside out—

The silver tint of the clouds of doubt,

And you never can tell how close you are,

It may be near when it seems so far;

So stick to the fight when you're hardest hit—

It's when things seem worst that you must not quit.

—Author Unknown

Adapt a winning attitude by developing a vocabulary that helps you create what you want. Do not talk yourself out of doing this part daily and often. Talk to yourself as much as needed to establish a new mindset, which will automatically take you in a different direction. When your vision is strong enough, stagnation no longer becomes an option. Your mind will move you in the direction of your vision if it is given a clear picture to operate from.

God designed us to work this way. What we talk about and what we see all day long is what we become. What do you see when you look in the mirror? That is who you are, and depending on your level of thinking, you can become or be whoever or whatever you want. Whether you have decided to be something, do something or not, you have made a decision. If you decide, then action steps will most likely follow. If you are undecided, stagnation will eliminate forward movement.

Ever run across a creek with no water flowing? What does it look like? Smell like? It is usually muddy with bugs and mosquitos buzzing around with a stale stench permeating throughout the air and no other sign of life. Now imagine a pond that has water flowing. It's absolutely full of life. There's fish, frogs and wildlife emanating all around. Well, this is very similar to what an idea does. It flows into your mind. It becomes a burning desire and, then, flows out in the way of a finished product. Now, that finished product can materialize into many other sources like notoriety, opportunities and, of course, added income. Once achieved, God gives you a fresh idea to work with so it flows in and then flows out, and the cycle continues.

God is a God of plenty, so there is an infinite supply of all that you need—good thoughts, ideas, money and whatever else is needed. Fear has no place to engage if action becomes a critical part of your life. Learn to confront your fear, and fear can't survive.

In May of 2012, I was diagnosed with Multiple Myeloma. At that time, I was told that my life could be extended eighteen to twenty-four months. I was not prepared to die. I remember being in a daze, almost numb. I had to make a decision right then and there to walk by faith and not by sight.

I had to take the diagnosis as fact, but I had to take God's word as truth. By His stripes I am healed. No weapon formed against me shall prosper. My wife wrote on a three-by-five card "No matter what it looks like, you are healed." She taped that card on my bathroom mirror for me to see day and night.

I got some more of those cards and wrote statements on them to read day and night: "Every cell in my body is healthy. I am healthy in mind, body and spirit. I am in perfect health." "I am an overcomer. I will live and not die." I would read these and more such statements every morning first thing and every night right before drifting off to sleep.

I continued to seek God's face for answers. I truly felt that the Holy Spirit would give me all the answers that I needed. I woke up very early one morning at about 4:00 a.m., and I got down on my knees and cried out to Almighty God. A voice came to me. "You are not trusting me." At first, I had no idea why I heard this statement, because I had always believed that I was truly trusting God in every area of my life, and yet again, I heard the voice. "You are not trusting me."

I was puzzled to the point and had to begin a process of evaluation about my walk with God. I pondered on this statement over the next few days. Again, I woke up very early just a few days later, and as I was praying, I hear this voice: "Stop taking chemotherapy." A great fear swept over me. I began to really think about the whole process and how it was affecting me.

As I was going through the painstaking process of chemotherapy, nothing seemed to be working to heal my body. I was getting worse and worse. I kept hearing that voice. "Stop taking chemotherapy."

As I was praying one morning, a question came to mind: *How can my body ever heal when I am being pumped with chemo medication every day? How can my cells regenerate if they are being killed every day?* It made absolutely no sense. I remember when I made a decision to stop taking my chemotherapy medicine. The fear of dying was overwhelming, but in order for me to live, that fear had to die. To let go of that fear, I had to face the fact that I could physically die. Knowing that made me take a long deep look at my own salvation. I had to know that I was grounded in the right stuff and that Heaven was my home. I had professed salvation over twenty years ago, and even so, I had to re-examine my heart and my own belief system about what Jesus had done on the cross.

Being 100 percent assured of my salvation also made me clearly understand that everything was based on what I believed about who I was and how God created me to win from the very beginning. How do I know that? He created us in His image after His likeness. Genesis 1:26 says, "Let us make man in our image, after our likeness: and let them have dominion over the fish of the sea, and over the fowl of the air, and over the cattle, and over all the earth, and over every creeping thing that creepeth upon the earth."

Not only did He make us in His image after His likeness, He also gave us dominion over everything, including all the earth. Now doesn't that mean that we were created to win? What about Psalm 8:4-5? "What is man, that thou art mindful of him? And the son of man, that thou visitest him? For thou hast made him a little lower than the angels, and hast crowned him with glory and honour." The word "fear" itself simply means "false evidence appearing real." I trusted my Spirit Man and stopped taking the chemotherapy treatments without the doctor's knowledge. I kept reading my statements day and night consistently.

I continued to make all my appointments as scheduled, and the doctors told me that the disease was not getting any worse. As time passed, they began to see improvement. Eventually, they wanted to check my blood levels to verify the extent of the disease. The Myeloma was getting better, and I began to feel better.

Finally, about six months had gone by and there was no sign of Myeloma in my bloodstream. The doctors wanted to be sure that what they were seeing was indeed a true indication of these Myeloma levels, so they ordered a bone biopsy. There was no Myeloma in my bone marrow. I was officially healed of Multiple Myeloma, and I haven't looked back since.

Fear is a lie, and it keeps many of us in bondage. This is another reason that Jesus died on the cross so that Satan would not have power over us through this gut-wrenching fear of death. I Corinthians 15:55-57 says, "O Death where is thy sting? O grave where is thy victory?" The sting of death is sin, and the strength of sin is the law.

But thanks be to God, who "giveth us the victory through our Lord Jesus Christ." This emotion of fear is an illusion and was not created of God. 2 Timothy says, "[7] For God hath not given us the spirit of fear; but of power, and of love, and of a sound mind." This is by far one of my favorite verses.

According to the Noah Webster's 1828 American Dictionary of the English Language, the definition of the word "fear" is "a painful emotion or passion excited by an expectation of evil, or the apprehension of impending danger." Fear expresses less apprehension than dread, and dread less than terror and fright. The force of this passion, beginning with the most moderate degree, may be thus expressed as fear, dread, terror, fright.

Fear is accompanied with a desire to avoid or ward off the expected evil. Fear is an uneasiness of the mind, upon the thought of future evil likely to befall us. Now consider this definition for just a moment. How is it possible for evil to come upon me if I give a speech in front of a thousand people or sing a song at a church convention? The fear is what I have created in my mind about speaking in front of a thousand people or singing at a church convention. It is not the act of what we do that frightens us. It is the response of those thousand people not giving the speech or singing the song that scares us. We are most afraid of not being accepted or approved by those in attendance. We are seeking to please the audience rather than focusing on giving a great speech or singing the song to the best of our God-given ability.

If we focus on the excellence of what we are providing rather than an imaginary assumption of what the audience might or might not think, then fear will have no place in us. Fear is an emotion mostly created out of unrealistic expectations either from us or those we are hoping to engage. When we take a long, hard look at the causes of fear, we will discover that we need to eliminate doubt, indecision and anxiety. One of these three emotions are usually responsible for creating fear. Doubt is feeling uncertain or unsure about something, whether it be because of a lack of knowledge or uncertainty about the outcome. All three of these emotions go hand and hand with fear.

Doubting strips us of our confidence and impedes our performance. Doubt can literally stop us in our tracks because the uncertainty is just too overwhelming. It also is a close cousin to indecision. Being undecided about something has the similarity of throwing your hands up in the air and quitting. Not deciding on something is the same as not doing anything, and not doing anything most often ends up having a negative impact.

Our biggest hurdle when dealing with indecisiveness is perfection. We don't want to make a poor decision because someone might criticize that decision. Criticisms can be very biased depending on the source. Most persons who are doing the criticizing are critiquing on the basis of their perspective and the roads they have traveled in life. Their ability to make decisions is based on their life's experiences and the perceptions created from them. Never concern yourself with someone else's viewpoint about decisions affecting your life.

The only persons you should consider are those that are directly affected by your decisions. Being responsible for others usually prompts us to make better decisions. We focus more on being responsible for a family and not just self. Learning to face our fears will eventually give us freedom. With this new-found freedom, we can experience things that expand our minds and elevate us to unforeseeable heights.

This freedom allows our creativity to flow, and the magnificence of God begins to show up in the way of new ideas, useful inventions and life-changing solutions for our communities and the world. We begin to give to those around us the talents and abilities that God has placed in us. We begin to spread our wings as eagles and fly at higher heights than ever before. We begin to go where few have ever gone and never will go. We have been released from this stagnant emotion called fear.

Finally, the greatest fear of all is the fear of death. We fear death because with death comes incompletion. Once we die, what's left undone can never be done. Every time fear stopped you in your tracks, it won. Every time fear allowed doubt to enter your mind, it won. Every time fear prevented you from launching that multi-million-dollar idea, it won. Every time fear convinced you to quit, it won. Every time you allowed fear, you lost. More importantly, those you love and the world around you, lost.

"False evidence appearing real" has ruled so many of us for so long that our God-given talents are never exposed. Then death comes along, and all those unrealized talents and abilities are buried. We can do nothing in the grave. Every dream never realized dies the moment you enter into death. All the ideas, all the missed opportunities, all those hopes and desires to do better are no more. Death comes to us all at some point. The Bible says that we all have an appointed time. That's why overcoming fear is so very important. Now is the time to do whatever it is that God put in you to do. Now is the only time that we really have.

Learn to operate in that moment of time and space called the present. Live the life you have imagined right now. We never know when death will come calling. It could come in the very next moment, so decide to make your journey right now. God has given us all that we need to be everything that we are. We are one of God's greatest creations, and He did not create us to be medio-cre. He designed unique systems with laws that help manifest our every desire.

CHAPTER FOUR

God Created Methods for Guaranteed Success

The laws of the universe will help us get anything we desire. God provided laws that work regardless of what we say or do. One of the most-talked-about laws is the law of gravity. What goes up must come down, because gravity will always do its job. It does not ask questions, and it won't deviate outside of its design. No matter who we are or how much wealth we've obtained, jump off a ten-story building and we will die just like the person who doesn't have a nickel to their name.

Everything God designed was put in place to serve us for an eternity, and those things had to do the same thing over and over no matter how often or for what person. The same laws that work for Bill Gates or Warren Buffet also work for you and me. The exact same formulas that's worked for others will work for anyone.

God put into place systems that work in the invisible realm. Everything starts in the unseen world before appearing in the physical world. Manifestation of our desires begin to formulate the very instant it is spoken. In other words, we get exactly what we confess with our mouth. When God speaks, there is a law associated with His Word. It was designed to bring forth whatever has been spoken. Remember back in the book of Genesis when God created the heavens and the earth. What does the Bible say? In every instance of creation, the verse began with "And God said," And then concluded with "And it was so."

Now think about the power of words if God created the Heaven and the earth with spoken words. Then that means words have a purpose, and that purpose is creation. Every word that we speak creates something, whether it be negative or positive; the law of creation still works. Our words are law and must bring forth what has been spoken. That's why some folks have exactly what they want in life while others get the total opposite. Why? Because everything we have in life depends on the words we have spoken.

When the Bible talks about God not being mocked, it is because God knows what He has designed and how His design works; therefore, what we say, good or bad, develops in our lives. If we are dead set on gossiping about someone in a bad way, then we are also gossiping about ourselves in that same manner. When we call someone else a jerk, we are also calling ourselves a jerk. When we make fun of someone else, we are actually making fun of ourselves with our own words. This is why the Bible says that

God can't be mocked. He designed words to do exactly what they were meant to, and that is, to create.

Why am I putting such emphasis on words and what we say? It is detrimental to our health, wealth and success. We must understand God's systems in order to reap the full benefits of what they all have to offer. Think about a system of automation. You are working in a factory that builds cars. Robots are created to do monotonous tasks over and over and over with precision exactly the same way day in and day out year after year. They are designed to work no matter who turns the machine on; they will do what they were designed to do. A child could turn them on, and they will work; an adult can do the same, and they will work. A man or a woman or any ethnic group can operate that machinery, and it will still do exactly what it is designed to do.

The same holds true with our choice of words. Whatever words we speak brings what we have spoken to life. Words really do matter. Control of our thoughts drives what we will speak. That is why the Bible says in Philippians 4:4, "Finally, brethren, whatsoever things are true, whatsoever things *are* honest, whatsoever things *are* just, whatsoever things *are* pure, whatsoever things *are* lovely, whatsoever things *are* of good report; if *there be* any virtue, and if *there be* any praise, think on these things." Why? Because the things that we think about is what will sooner or later flow out of our mouth.

There are other laws that God has put in place to help us get the things that we want in life, and in order to utilize them, we must first know what they are and how they work. Knowledge alone is never enough to bring about lasting change. Wisdom comes not from knowing, but having the diligence to do what we know. Understanding does not come from gathering information, but by acting on that information. How do we act on what we know? We must first develop a strong desire for positive change.

Like anything else in life, desire can be created through discipline and perseverance. Redesigning yourself takes a tremendous amount of effort. Starting over will always have its challenges, and putting in the work very rarely seems appealing. However, the results are well worth the effort, and the time put into life-changing transition will pay huge dividends. Results don't lie, and change is eminent if you put in the work.

Arnold Schwarzenegger dreamed of becoming Mr. Universe. He wrapped his whole mind and body into what he imagined himself to be, until one day, he became that which he wanted to be. He didn't do it sitting on the couch and hoping for it to happen. There was more than just wishing and praying. He put in years of rigorous work to develop and sculpt his body into Mr. Universe.

We can only become what we want to be once we have decided to be what we want to be. The Bible talks about calling those things that be not as though they were. We will never be until we have become. Now what does this mean? Imagine that you want to be a world-renowned author. You dream about it day and night, but deep down you doubt that you have the abilities necessary to become a writer. Until you believe that you are an author, you will never be an author because you must first become what it is that you desire to be. Once you have resolved in your own mind that you are an author, you will be an author.

Like anything, starting is the most difficult part. To be an author, you must first sit down and begin to write. You must find a way to put ink to paper for the formulation of ideas. Don't concern yourself with what you know or don't know; just empty your thoughts on paper. You'll be utterly surprised at the end result. I read a lot of John Maxwell who writes excellent books on leadership. In his book *The Fifteen Invaluable Laws of Growth,* he states that "you must be before you can do." Now many of us can't conceive being something that we aspire to be, because in our own minds, we have no clue how to become what it is that we want to be.

God created our imagination for one reason only—so we could be whatever we choose to be in that imaginary world and, at some point, the imagination can easily translate into reality. We must first imagine ourselves as that person that we want to be. Then, we must believe with every fiber of our being that what we have imagined is exactly who we are.

Think back when we were children and we were out in the yard playing with our friends. As children, our imaginations ran absolutely rampant. We could pretend to be the king of England or the Prince of Wales or even the president of the United States, and whatever we pretended to be is exactly what we became in our very own little world. No one could tell us that we were not any of those things.

That is exactly why Jesus alludes to having the faith of a child. Children believe that they can be anything they imagine until they are inundated with worldviews and human fears. Our imaginations are powerful and can catapult us into a new way of life if only we let it. For some reason, we all grow up and forget about the one tool that instantly changes us from who we are to who we want to be.

Imagine yourself in a dark room. Now no matter how hard you try, you can't see your hand in front of your face. Then someone comes along and flips on a light switch, and the sudden brightness of light hurts your eyes. But eventually, your vision comes into focus, and you can now see everything in the room. Well, new information works very similarly.

We hear something that goes against beliefs that have been thoroughly ingrained in us for as long as we can remember. The shock of this new information stings a little, like the effect of that bright light on the eyes. Now the mind deciphers the information to determine whether it makes sense. Remember the Spirit Man knows all things. The truth will always be revealed to us. A peace will come over us. Now we have been exposed to another mechanism designed to help us achieve our every desire.

God has not made anything too difficult for us. All of these are simple laws created to serve us, yet we spar over them as if though they are a curse rather than a blessing. Paul tells us that "the things I know to do I do not." Many of us know about these mechanisms, and yet we do not abide by what we know. Why? Because the majority operates in the Babylonian system, and the world system will never give us what God intended. God makes it clear in His Word that we reap what we sow.

Reaping and sowing are not only associated with finances or abundance. We also reap what we sow in the way of words and the context that we use them in. Words are the pinnacle to our overall success. Our health, wealth and success are all centered on how and what we say. The bottom line is that our words and the faith that we carry behind those words, as created by God, are key to our success. As I have mentioned in previous chapters, God is a creator. The book of John Chapter 1 talks about how in the beginning was the Word and the Word was with God and the Word was God.

Now if the Word was God and God created all things to include us, and He created us in His image after His likeness, then the Word must be incredibly significant in all that we become. If we don't like ourselves, we should change our words. If our life is not what we would like it to be, we should change our words. If our marriage is in shambles and our finances in disarray, then we should change our words.

Life is shaped by the law of our words. Pastor Bill Winston gave a teaching on the law of confession. And one of the things that he strongly emphasized was, "We have not made the connection between what we say and what we get and that no one ever rises above their confession." Now this is a very powerful statement. Everything we confess with our mouth starts happening in our life the very instant we finish our sentence. Just think for one moment how much we have created that we did not want because of what we have said. For when we speak without the knowledge of what we are creating, our lives will constantly flow towards the negative rather than the positive. For what we have placed in our heart by the words of our mouth will continue to rule our lives and provide us no clear direction.

I want you to imagine going on a cruise to Jamaica. You get on the ship, and you discover that the captain has directions, but to the Cayman Islands. You've always dreamed of going to Jamaica. How did the captain get directions for the Cayman Islands? Because what you dreamed and what you said were not the same. You dreamed of going to Jamaica, but you said that the Cayman Islands would be a great place to venture off to.

Now the rudder is what guides the ship, and yet, it is the smallest part of all the mechanisms designed to move that ship. The ship can only go if the rudder is properly functioning. Without it, the ship does not move and it certainly does not go where it is supposed to. Now imagine that our tongues or the words spoken with our tongue are the rudder. If our rudder is not speaking our lives in the direction that our dreams envision, then it is clear that we are not speaking what we are dreaming. We are only speaking what we have limited ourselves to having.

Oftentimes, we think more about what others think about our dreams and remain fearful to share our dreams, so we choose not to talk about what others may not understand. Therefore, we only speak on those things that are acceptable to the masses, and we forego our inner desires for the sake of the whole. But in all that sacrifice, we come to discover that the whole only knows in part, because God knows what He has designed in us. The Bible clearly states that God gives us the desires of our heart. So why let fear and conformity prevent us from speaking what God has placed in us?

We look to be respected by those who don't respect themselves. How then can they offer us what they can't even give themselves? We must be confident in the house that God built. Every trial, tribulation, sacrifice and condition that your life has been laced with has shaped the very fiber that molded just you. When the mold is broken, there is no other compared to who you have become.

Travel down the chosen road alone if you must, but step by step, you will arrive at the end and there waiting for you is victory. Regardless of what the majority thought as you were travelling, when you get to the end of the road, they will now understand that you were going somewhere that they were not prepared to go. Our lives are clearly directed by the words of our mouth. We will boldly talk about what we believe, and it will never matter what others think about what they can't understand. A lot of times we believe that others have a right to direct our lives according to the fears that they live by.

Overcoming our own fears takes enough work as it is, so contemplating what directions we should take to achieve our dreams based on others insecurities is like diving out of a plane with no parachute. There is no way to safely land at our destination without the comfort of knowing that we have opened our parachute.

Eaglets must be pushed out of the security of their nest before realizing that they alone can spread their wings and fly. God has equipped us to be able to fly, and many of us let our thoughts hinder us from spreading our wings. Many believe that, once a person reaches a certain age, they should be endowed with wisdom. Yet, time in years is not the measuring stick for wisdom, because wisdom comes from God. A twenty-year-old could be wiser than an eighty-year-old.

Age in the Kingdom of God is irrelevant. God can use the young or the old. Never judge another person's character on the basis of your own character. You can't force someone to come up to your level of knowledge or wisdom, for what you have sought after and received of God was bestowed upon you by your seeking. Not everyone in your circle of life is travelling down the same roads you have chosen. For the road that you have travelled and the person that God has molded you into prepared you for all you have received.

Remember the story that I shared earlier about the pumpkin that was placed in a small jar. The pumpkin grew to the size of that small jar and could grow no more. But when removed from that small jar and placed in a much larger jar, the pumpkin then expanded and grew to the size of that much-larger jar. You can only receive what you have grown into. This is why continuous learning and education are so critical.

Reading the Bible and getting it down inside your spirit will fill you with the wisdom and knowledge about what to do next. Reading the right books dramatically adds the best concepts to your arsenal. The Bible says in Proverbs 4:7 that "wisdom is the principal thing; therefore, get wisdom, and with all thy getting get understanding." Ecclesiastes 7:12 states, "For wisdom is a defense, and money is a defense; but the Excellency of knowledge is, that wisdom giveth life to them that have it."

Now how do we obtain wisdom? We ask this of God. The book of James Chapter 1 Verse 5 says, "If any of you lack wisdom, let him ask of God, that giveth to all men liberally, and upbraideth not; and it shall be given him. But let him ask in faith, nothing wavering. For he that wavereth is like a wave of the sea driven with the wind and tossed. For let not that man think that he shall receive anything of the Lord. A double-minded man is unstable in all his ways."

Like anything in life done with any significance, a decision has to be made to seek that which you desire with intentionality and focus. Life will only hand out what you expect. If you expect little, then you will get little, and if you expect great things, then you will receive great things. Our God in Heaven is not a small God, and He did not give us a small mind. If you are going to hold a thought in your mind for change, it might as well be a thought big enough for our God to deliver. Why spend time asking for a Ford Focus when you can use the exact same energy asking for a Rolls Royce? Even if you fall short of getting the Rolls Royce and end up in a Mercedes S Class or a BMW S series, you still ranked up purely by changing your thinking—same energy, different result.

God has created different laws that produce exact outcomes for every aspect of our lives. What I am about to present is not something that will be popular among most, and yet, this is not my creation but God's. We have absolutely no problem discussing some of God's laws like the law of gravity or the law of relativity. Now as large as the universe is, why would God have only created a few laws for such mass to fluidly operate every second of every day each and every year for eternity? The universe is a very huge expanse that goes on and on for light years. Surely, God in all His infinite wisdom would have created laws that hold all this together and function as He designed without fail.

There are a few other laws that are relevant to us when it comes to getting the things we want in life: the law of attraction, the law of compensation and the law of perpetual transmutation of energy. They all fit very well in this discussion of God putting things in place for our guaranteed success. Like any law that God has put in place, they all work on the basis of the law of confession. Every law is interconnected, and they work as a team.

Everything functions in God's universe depending on our creative words. What we speak sets a lot of stuff in motion like God's laws. For instance, once we confess what it is that we are expecting, invisible forces go to work to bring the very things our words have spoken into manifestation. Our thoughts produce a belief. That belief is then trickled down to the heart, and then the mouth speaks what is in the heart. Once the mouth speaks and the words go forth, every law starts doing their specific part to create what has been spoken.

The law of confession confesses what belief comes from the heart. The law of attraction draws the resources and connections necessary to move you towards what you have spoken. It draws unto itself the thoughts and things that are identical to it. Whatever you give your attention to will manifest in your life. This is how the law of attraction works. The law of compensation starts formulating the amount of pay that is equivalent to what your word has identified as your worth. The law of perpetual transmutation of energy then goes to work manifesting the desired objects from the invisible world to the natural world.

Every law in existence was created by God before He placed Adam and Eve in the garden. It should come as no surprise that God implemented laws and systems that perfectly accommodates His creation. Jesus understood these laws and adequately used them just as God designed. God has made us accountable for seeking and gaining understanding, and His laws and statutes are part of His complete and perfect plan.

Most of us dismiss what we cannot comprehend or have not yet gained an understanding of. I have no clue where God came from, and no understanding of the overall power that God possesses. Regardless, by faith, I believe without question that He exists. I have not a clue how the earth hangs and spins on its axis, and yet, I clearly understand that there are intricate mathematical laws at work making sure that it hangs at a precise angle and rotates at a certain speed indefinitely. The laws that hang the stars in the sky and rotate the earth around the sun, I have zero understanding of, yet there hang the stars, and sunrise and sunset happen like clockwork each and every day.

Not understanding something has no merit when it comes to its existence. Lack of understanding has never affected the validity of something. The truth remains whether we can decipher what it means or how it works. These laws are there as tools to assist us in speaking our lives into the realities that we choose. We don't have to fear what we don't understand, but we should fear refusal to seek knowledge beyond what we know. Compared to the enormity of God's overall creation, we know only in part what makes the whole.

God did not create man to live a lowly, unhappy, dismal existence. He created us to be conquerors, overcomers and creators. We can create anything that we want by absorbing all the knowledge that we can pertaining to the mysteries of God. We could spend an entire lifetime seeking knowledge and understanding and never even come close to the realization of what God has really done.

In order for us to absorb more, we must broaden our viewpoints enough to allow new information in. If we choose to have a closed mind and hold strict views, we can only grow to the limit that those views will allow. When we open our minds to other possibilities that are unfamiliar or uncomfortable to our way of thinking, we offer ourselves an opportunity to stimulate our growth.

Success looks like many things to different people. Some feel successful being healthy and having family in their lives. Others feel that success is having everything they desire including health, family and abundance. Many don't value those things at all and are quite happy just existing. Any avenue that a person has chosen to epitomize success is fine as long as it is moral, legal and bears no harm to other human beings.

Since we are eternal beings, everything we do must have eternity in mind. Our life is but a vapor and is over in the blink of an eye. This is why it is imperative to plan our lives because our time here on earth is short compared to eternity. God expects us to plan our lives well. Proverbs 13:22 says a good person leaves an inheritance for their children's children, but a sinner's wealth is stored up for the righteous. God has given us all the tools we need to build and leave a legacy for our children and grandchildren. After all, the scripture shows that God chose us, and He appointed us to go bear fruit. In John 15:16, God says, "You did not choose me, but I chose you and appointed you that you should *go and bear fruit* and that *your fruit should abide*, so that whatever you ask the Father in my name, he may give it to you."

There are four key elements in this verse. First, God chose us. Ephesians 1:5 says, "According as he hath chosen us in him before the foundation of the world, that we should be holy and without blame before him in love: having predestinated us unto the adoption of children by Jesus Christ to himself, according to the good pleasure of his will." Now since God has chosen us, He would have also equipped us with the necessary tools to bear fruit. What are those tools? Our God has given us talents and abilities. Whatever God has placed in you was provided as a gift to serve others. This gift or gifts will also bring you into your wealthy place. Proverbs 18:16 says, "A man's gift maketh room for him, and bringeth him before great men." Then in Matthew 25:29, God says, "For unto every one that hath shall be given, and he shall have abundance: but from him that hath not shall be taken away even that which he hath." Why would God give to those who already have, and take away from those who have not?

Remember the parable that Jesus illustrated about the talents? Their master was about to embark upon a long journey. He had three servants whom he entrusted with his goods. To one he gave five talents, to another he gave two, and to another, one: to every man according to his ability. Then the master straightway took his journey. Now, as the story goes, the one with five talents traded with the same and earned five more. Likewise, the one with two also earned another two, but he that received one went and dug a hole in the earth and hid his lord's money. The master returned from his journey and enquired of each servant. The one with five talents earned and additional five talents for a total of ten talents. Similarly, the servant with two talents also gained two more talents for a total of four talents. The servant with one talent was afraid and hid his lord's talent in the earth and returned to his master one talent. His lord answered and said to him, "You wicked and slothful servant, you knew that I reaped where I sowed not, and gathered where I have not strewn; you should have therefore put my money to the exchangers and then at my coming I should have received my own with usury. Take therefore the talent from him and give it unto him which hath ten talents. For unto every one that hath shall be given, and he shall have abundance; but from him that hath not shall be taken away even that which he hath."

Now think for a moment about how this story plays out. Why did the man with more talents double his talents to ten and the other servant do the same with his two talents? And why was the one servant with only one talent looked at so differently by his master? After all, he did not lose his master's talent. He protected it. Why did the master construe the servant with the one talent as wicked and slothful? Well, there are many ways to decipher this parable, but in terms of Kingdom principles, God has a purpose for our lives and our talents.

The servants that doubled their talents used the abilities within them and took risks to double their master's money. The servant with one talent was fearful of using his abilities to produce a return on his lord's money, which required giving nothing of himself. In the Kingdom of God, we are all housed with an innate talent or ability. Some of us have several talents or abilities, but for those who have them, God expects us to use them to nurture and grow the Kingdom. 1 Peter 4:10-11 says, "As each has received a gift, use it to serve one another, as good stewards of God's varied grace: whoever speaks, as one who speaks oracles of God; whoever serves, as one who serves by the strength that God supplies—in order that in everything God may be glorified through Jesus Christ. To him belongs glory and dominion forever and ever. Amen."

Romans 12:6-8 says, "Having gifts that differ according to the grace given to us, let us use them: if prophecy, in proportion to our faith; if service, in our serving; the one who teaches, in his teaching; the one who exhorts, in his exhortation; the one who contributes, in generosity; the one who leads, with zeal; the one who does acts of mercy, with cheerfulness."

God did not give us these talents and abilities to keep them to ourselves. Everything we do every single day should grow the Kingdom in some way. Whether we spend time enhancing and continuing to perfect what God has placed in us, or passing on our gifts to teach, inspire or advance others, we should understand the significance of empowering the children of God. We never know what is kindling within the soul of our brother or sister. One word of encouragement might be the last piece that ignites and displays God's hidden treasure within them.

We are given a critical assignment during our short-lived existence here on earth. We are to carry out the will of God, because in the end of our days, what we gathered over our lifetime will become rubble; therefore, only what we do for Christ will last. If we sow in abundance, giving our life to others, then we will reap bountifully. This is how wealth is accumulated in the Kingdom of God. Every minute of every waking day should be focused on how to expand the Kingdom here on earth.

I have often heard people say that one person can't make a difference. I remember a savior named Jesus that made a difference. How about a man by the name of Martin Luther King Jr.? I say he made a difference. A woman by the name of Harriet Tubman, sick and tired of the bonds and detriments of slavery, decided to risk her life to rise up contrary to the status quo, against what seemed insurmountable odds to help free black slaves. How about Moses who led over 4 million slaves out of the grips of bondage from the most powerful civilization on earth? Our one life makes more of a difference than what we will really ever know.

Our existence alone has impacted someone else's life in some way, somehow, without our ever even knowing it. God created us for a purpose. Our life has meaning even if we are unable to see who we have touched or how deeply. God knows who He has placed us here for, and every time we are in the presence of others, we have an opportunity to extend God's grace to someone else in the way of gentleness, encouragement and genuine compassion. Our light shines by how we act towards others. Love your neighbor as yourself, is the Golden Rule. God gave us perfect insights on how to treat one another. Like any good father, He left us a set of instructions and principles to live by. He also selected us to do something.

The second part of that verse in John 15:16 is that He appointed us to go and bear fruit. Being appointed to something means that it has been predetermined or prearranged. Ambassadors are appointed by the president of the United States. They are placed in a foreign country as the chief executives responsible for all federal employees under their jurisdiction. They also represent the United States in that foreign land. So, God appointed us to go and bear fruit. Where did He appoint us to go? Wherever He calls, according to the unction of the Holy Spirit. We limit ourselves to where we live, but to God, the entire earth is his embassy and we go where He instructs us to go.

He gave man dominion over all the earth and everything in the earth; therefore, our jurisdiction is planet earth. When we go where God tells us to go, and once we get there, we are to bear fruit. There are many ways to bear fruit. We can let the goodness of God within us flow out of us into the lives of those around us. We can aid those in need, whether it be emotionally, spiritually or physically. Some may need to be consoled after losing a lifelong partner, brother, sister or friend. Others may need spiritual guidance on their newfound journey of following Jesus Christ. Others may need shelter, clothing, transportation or something to eat. Whatever the need is, we are to let our light shine and be the provider of that need.

In order to see what is evident around us, we must have a compassionate eye so that we can recognize someone else's need. How do we develop compassion for others? We must first grow past our own shortcomings and insecurities. This is why it is so critical to live a life of constant and consistent self-evaluation to further our growth in every area of life.

"Judge not, that ye be not judged. For with what judgment ye judge, ye shall be judged: and with what measure ye mete, it shall be measured to you again. And why beholdest thou the mote that is in thy brother's eye, but considerest not the beam that is in thine own eye? Or how wilt thou say to thy brother, 'Let me pull out the mote out of thine eye'; and, behold, a beam is in thine own eye? Thou hypocrite, first cast out the beam out of thine own eye; and then shalt thou see clearly to cast out the mote out of thy brother's eye."

—Matthew 7:1-5

We must grow closer to our Lord and Savior who will guide us and lead us in all things; therefore, our Spiritual Man must be well fed. Our feeding ground is prayer and the Word of God. This will give us the strength to overcome our own life's battles, and have enough left to stand by others who do not yet have the strength to fight on their own.

God put us here as conduits for one another, and like always, there is strength in numbers and unity. Everything we need can be found within each other. This is one of the key mechanisms for success. Using each other's strengths to offset our own weaknesses is by God's great design. Remember the story about the Tower of Babel? The whole world had one language and a common speech. As people moved eastward, they found a plain in Shinar and settled there. They said to each other, "Come, let's make bricks and bake them thoroughly." They used brick instead of stone, and tar for mortar. Then they said, "Come, let us build ourselves a city, with a tower that reaches to the heavens, so that we may make a name for ourselves; otherwise we will be scattered over the face of the whole earth." But the Lord came down to see the city and the tower the people were building. The Lord said, "If as one people speaking the same language they have begun to do this, then nothing they plan to do will be impossible for them." This is the magic of creation. We are all one, and we complement one another.

There are other systems unique to our success: planning systems, spiritual systems, financial systems, business systems and personal systems. All of these systems work in conjunction with one another to provide a full and joyful life. Each of these systems must be designed according to your goals and expectations. Many of us plan for a day, week, maybe even a month or two. However, most successful people plan for the long term, as much as twenty years out. Then they plan annual goals that lead them to the achievement of their long-range goals. This is a much different perspective than the traditional day-to-day or month-to-month goal setting.

According to Benjamin Franklin, big achievements come one small advantage at a time. Learning and understanding the power of baby steps are what ultimately lead us to greater and more significant rewards. Imagine a twenty-year-old person who makes plans to be a very successful, financially stable business owner retired at age forty. A twenty-year plan may seem like an eternity, but time has its way of passing by rather quickly. His chances of achieving this are far more realistic because he has properly planned and given himself a reasonable, doable timeline.

To think big and to achieve big, we must be willing to change something in our daily actions. Once we have disciplined ourselves to make the necessary changes, we must incorporate a habit of consistency. Deciding to make a dramatic change is just the first step in the transformation. Now that change has to occur long enough to become habit-forming. Until it becomes a part of your daily routine, it will be short-lived and eventually become non-existent. Falling back into a lifelong way of life is very easy to do. Most of us normally revert to what is comfortable.

Successful people know and understand that the fruit of their labor shows up when living in the realm of the uncomfortable. Challenging yourself to constantly do what you do not like to do will make all the difference in your journey to excel. The roads that you travel may seem bumpy at times. You may feel like you have taken all that you are able. You're frustrated and unsure of knowing whether or not you will ever see what you have imagined. There is one challenge after another and keeping that vision in front of you during tough times gets harder and harder, but know this—things are happening and doors are opening in the background, and your future is materializing piece by piece even if it is not visible to you yet. It soon will be, so find whatever it is that will drive you to keep going. Find it, wrap yourself around it and use it, because quitting regardless of how hard it may seem should never be a consideration until your vision has come to full fruition.

Winners never quit, and quitters never win. Your success is garnered around your ability to continue to move forward regardless of life's circumstances. Your circumstances do not define you. Know in your heart of hearts that life will happen, so you might as well decide to keep winning rather than give in to losing. Pitfalls will come, and unexpected events will happen. None of that matters. Those things will come to those doing great things as well as those who are not. God has put in all of us the ability to decide, and it is deciding that will ultimately propel you to the level you have imagined.

Procrastination is the enemy of decision. Putting things off until later or the next day means that it most likely will never get completed. Many of us have fallen victim to this all-too-popular habit of putting things off until some later date. I've done it more than I'd like to admit, and every single time, it has cost me. How many of you have said these exact words, "Oh I'm exhausted. I'll do that tomorrow.", "I don't want to take the time to learn that now. It's too hard.", "I don't like speaking in front of people. That's not my thing.", "They do that so well. I could never do that."? And the debilitating self-doubt goes on and on. Every time we put something off, we take a chance of never getting it done. "I've been in school all my life. I want to take a breather. I can go back to college anytime." Twenty years later, still no college degree.

Now in order to achieve what you could have done twenty years prior will take a whole lot more effort. Why? Because you're an adult with a wife and two kids. One is in high school and the other about to head off to college. Now your hindrance is going to be juggling family life, marriage, teenage kids and bills, lots of bills. The challenge to enroll, focus and be a successful student is not impossible, but improbable. You now have major responsibilities and other priorities. Because of your past decisions, your future now looks a little different than what you imagined. You have a family now. Things are expensive. You can't get a promotion to a higher end position because they require a college degree.

Now what? Do you start your own business? Do you hope that someone will give you an opportunity by overriding company guidelines to promote you? Do you wish upon a star or pray that some miracle happens? Or do you expect God to intervene and open a door for you somehow someway? As children of God, we know that anything is possible through Jesus Christ, but what about our responsibility? God is our father, and He provides our every need. The key word here is "need." Just like a child that you have nurtured all their lives to get them to the point of maturity to be able to live life on their own, God is no different. At some point, we have to use what God has placed inside of us to live the life that we want to live. We should not expect God to hand us a life that we have imagined on a silver platter. He has given us all the tools that we need to create whatever life we choose. It all starts and ends with decisions.

Every single decision you make or don't make matters. Putting things off until tomorrow is easy, but costly. It is a habit that gets easier and easier over time, and it becomes more and more detrimental to your ever having a chance to succeed. Procrastination creates the thought process that you have time to do it later. Your expectation is to have another day to get it done. What if your tomorrow never comes? What you could have completed today definitely won't ever get completed in death. When we really get the revelation that tomorrow may never come, we will live life with a sense of urgency like never before. We must get to a point where we understand that our flesh is not guaranteed another day. Choosing to live your life to the fullest in this moment puts you on a road that few will ever travel.

Think in terms of having a successful life today. I have a happy marriage today. I enjoy my world today. I am travelling to the places I want to go today. I choose not to live beyond the moment that I am in because I have no control of the moment after nor the moment past. As Joel Osteen said, "I am living my best life now."

I have no idea what it will take for many of you out there to get the revelation of living life now, but for me, it took a doctor telling me that I had eighteen to twenty-four months to live. Having someone tell you that your life is ending really gives you a hard slap in the face, because now, without a doubt, the most devastating revelation is that I have not lived my life to the best of my potential. God in his infinite mercy decided to change my destiny. It has now been eight years since I was told those words of a morbid fate. I relive that statement in my mind every time I feel the notion to quit. It is a solid reminder that tomorrow is not promised and we have no guarantees that we will complete anything tomorrow.

The most critical point that I can emphasize to those of you who are reading this book—the habits you develop will determine the life you live. You have total control over the habits you decide to create. Decide to discover your purpose. The process of daily self-reflection is to determine what you are doing or not doing to identify your true purpose. The habits you create should be formed around your purpose. More importantly, from this day on, understand that it is your choices that determine how you are going to live this life.

CHAPTER FIVE

Wealth Is Not an Accident

There is a scientific method to obtaining wealth. Like many laws that God created, He made a few to bring wealth into our lives. One of the most key laws for bringing wealth into our lives has to do with the words we speak. The law of confession coupled with belief will change your life in every area. This law used in conjunction with unwavering faith will produce whatever you say. Whether you speak positively or negatively, like the law of gravity, all laws just work. The old saying that you will have what you say holds true with this law.

The law of confession is evident in your life regardless of where you live or how you live. If you are living in a constant state of need, then you have created that lifestyle. If you can barely move around in your house because you have a hard time letting things go, then you created that environment. If every time you turn around you are struggling with finances, paying bills or saving money, then you are attracting this scarcity. Somewhere along the way, you have spoken what you are living, and by your speaking, you have come into agreement and found a way to be satisfied with your current situation. Everything you have or don't have clearly demonstrates the language that you have been speaking.

The events and people that come into our lives were attracted to us by the very things we have said. Every thought, word and action produces energies that attract like energies. Negative energies attract that same energy, just as positive energy attracts positive energy. If your life has not ended up like you expected, look no further than the mirror on the wall because that person is the only one that has the power to change your life.

Be accountable for your own thoughts, words and actions. The minute you look outside yourself for change is the very moment that you have decided to remain in the life you're living. In his book *The 15 Invaluable Laws of Growth*, John Maxwell states, "I have always been more motivated by the possibility of success than by the fear of failure." When you are more motivated by the possibilities of success rather than the fear of failure, your language will evolve into what is necessary to achieve whatever it is that you want in life. Once you have taken control of your thoughts and mastered your words, you will automatically begin to transition from not having enough to having more than you could ever imagine. The law of confession and the power of faith work hand in hand.

The law of confession, simply stated, are the words we speak in faith. Another thing that happens when we learn to speak correctly is cause and effect. What exactly is cause and effect? For every action, there is a reaction. When you drop a ball from a ten-story building, gravity reacts by pulling that ball towards the earth's center, and it will eventually hit the ground. When you lash out in anger and lose control, the reaction is to spew out negative, destructive statements that have no relevance in advancing your life. When you speak a word true or untrue, the reaction is that you get exactly what you say. The words we speak work in tandem with the law of attraction. The law of attraction brings to us those things that we have faithfully desired. The visible effects are the deeds provided to us in the way of gifts, money, inheritances, friendships and blessings. Meaning that the words we speak create an avenue for us to receive more than just better conditions or a changed attitude.

Something else that comes along with that are different forms of compensation. Most of us get up every day, drag ourselves out of bed before we really want to get up, get dressed and go to a job. Some of us love what we do and many of us hate what we do, but we do it to pay bills so that we can eat, buy clothes, support our families and have a nice, warm place to sleep at night. But more importantly, we do it in exchange for money. If we were not compensated, most of us would opt out of going to work every day.

Imagine if you could, just for a moment, realize that our words not only provide peace of mind, a better attitude and create nicer conditions, but they also will provide compensation. Have you ever gotten unexpected checks in the mail? How about gifts from some-one that you hardly even know? What about an inheritance from some uncle, aunt, grandparent or family member that you had no clue about? Ever had someone bless you with money when you least expected it? And how about some of those amazing friendships that have begun developing in your life? All of these things are occurring because of what you have been saying, and every one of them is a form of compensation.

The law of attraction works alongside the law of compensation to create the new life that you have now spoken into existence. Everything we do in life comes with a price. It does not matter what we decide to do or not to do; either way, we will be compensated with abundance and overflow or lack and destitution. But make no mistake—we reap what we sow.

Fertilize the garden of your mind with strong money principles and remain diligent so that you will reap what you have sown. According to the Word of God, "Money answers all matters."

"A feast is made for laughter, and wine maketh merry: but money answereth all things."

—Ecclesiastes 10:19 KJV

"Wealth gotten by vanity shall be diminished: but he that gathereth by labour shall increase."

—Proverbs 12:11 KJV

"He becometh poor that dealeth with a slack hand: but the hand of the diligent maketh rich."

—Proverbs 1:4 KJV

Money in itself will never buy joy or happiness. Having money will not prevent illnesses or catastrophes. It will not curtail unexpected events from occurring in life nor make someone love you. But money does help solve many everyday problems. When you have an abundance of wealth, things like cars breaking down, heating and cooling issues or paying bills don't hold the same concerns as a household where money is tight.

I adopted a key principle about money a long time ago. It is simply a tool or commodity that you exchange for the things you want. When you look at money as a tool, your whole approach about how to handle money dramatically changes. There is no longer a need to hoard it or put it somewhere in a hidden safe never to be circulated.

Money is best served flowing in and out of your life. It must circulate to give you the best benefit. Everything in the Kingdom of God is predicated on one key principle: sowing and reaping. Money is no different. You sow by giving, and you reap from what you have sown; therefore, sow bountifully so that you may reap bountifully.

In the book *The Richest Man in Babylon*, there is a story of a rich man. He was well known throughout the region for his great wealth. The rich man was very generous giving to various charities. He was generous with his family. He was lavish with spending in his own household. Yet, each year his wealth increased regardless of how much he had spent.

One day, the rich man was approached by a childhood friend who said to him, "You are more fortunate than we. You have become the richest man in Babylon while we struggle for existence. You wear the finest garments and you enjoy the rarest foods yet we struggle to provide our basic needs.

"You and I were once equal. We studied under the same teachers at the same schools. We played together on the same playgrounds. You were no better of a student than anyone else and up until now, you have not been a more model citizen.

"You have not worked any harder or been more faithful as far as we can see. Why then should fate be so gracious as to afford you such a grand life and unjustly ignore all the rest of us?"

The rich man paused and patiently assessed what had been said. He responded, "If you have not managed to gain more than a mere existence since we were children, it is because you have failed to understand the laws that govern how to obtain wealth, or else you simply do not observe them."

After hearing the words of the rich man, another friend of their youth, who was poor, approached him. He had trouble understanding what he must do to turn his financial situation around. He thought that, if he could just earn more, everything would be alright. The amount he earned had nothing to do with his current situation. It was his attitude about money and how to use it. He observed a rich man who lived on the other end of the village, and they had great wealth and abundance. He wanted to have that same lifestyle.

He began to inquire of the rich man about some of the principles that he lived by to obtain such great wealth. The rich man told him that he had to find a way to become the lender to the borrower.

This was one way to start building wealth. The money that you lend will gain usury and will work in your favor.

The rich man then told him about a basic principle that would help guarantee a solid building block towards creating wealth. This is what he told the poor man:

1. *Save 10 percent of all that you earn and this you do not touch.*

2. *Save 10 percent for unexpected emergencies and mishaps.*

3. *Save 10 percent for investments and opportunities.*

4. *Decide to live on the 70 percent, and you will eventually see great increase.*

The young man, thanks to this advice, eventually went on to become one of the richest men in Babylon. The principles that the rich man shared are principles that work just as well today as they did back then. I have been using these principles for a very long time in my life and have experienced great results. However, I am a born-again believer, and for me, there was a small caveat.

1. *Tithe 10 percent to the church for the work of the Kingdom.*

2. *Save 10 percent of all that you earn, and do not touch it.*

3. *Save 10 percent for unexpected emergencies.*

4. *Save 10 percent for investments and other opportunities.*

5. *Decide to live on the remaining 60 percent.*

Both of these examples are just basic guidelines. You can adjust this to your situation. For instance, you may only be able to save 5 percent or less for each category and that's fine. Don't get hung up on the amount. It is the principle that's important. Follow these principles, and your life will never be the same. Living in scarcity will become a thing of the past, and you will eventually take control of your finances.

God has created perfect systems that were designed to work effectively and efficiently for eternity. The more we learn about what He has designed, the quicker we can reap the benefits.

How many of you believe that there is an invisible world that is far greater in size and depth than the physical world? Everything exists in the invisible world, including God. A great man of God visited our church and delivered a life-changing sermon. During this sermon, he told us that faith is the currency that brings things from the invisible world to the physical world. Like the law of gravity, the law of attraction and the law of compensation, there is a law that brings things into manifestation from the invisible world to the physical world. This law is called the law of perpetual transmutation of energy.

The law of perpetual transmutation of energy states that all persons have within them the power to change the conditions of their lives. Higher vibrations consume and transform lower ones; thus, each of us can change the energies in our lives by understanding the laws that God has put in place and applying the principles in such a way as to effect change. In the world of religion, this is a very sensitive subject. Why? For some reason, many believe that these laws are something separate from God's creation; yet, many have no issues with easily discussing the law of gravity, the law of relativity, the law of attraction and the law of confession with little to no disagreements. God has told us in his Word to seek knowledge and wisdom, but more importantly, gain understanding. Proverbs 4:7 says, "Wisdom is the principal thing; therefore get wisdom: and with all thy getting get understanding."

In order to gain more understanding than what we have, our minds must be open to concepts that we may not initially agree with. We may not even understand what is being said at the moment or why. This is one of the reasons why thinking has to be re-instituted into our everyday lives. Just sitting down, alone, in a dark room with absolute quiet allows the Holy Spirit to guide you. All that you have sought after will be revealed. If knowledge and wisdom are your principle goal, then God will give you revelation in your quiet time.

Nothing happens by accident in the Kingdom of God. The roads that you travel have all been paved by Almighty God. The relationships you build, the people you encounter, the situations you happen to find yourself in, the ideas, inventions, talents and abilities are all from above.

"Every good gift and every perfect gift is from above, and cometh down from the Father of lights, with whom is no variableness, neither shadow of turning. Of his own will begat he us with the word of truth, that we should be a kind of first fruits of his creatures."

—James 1:17 KJV

That's why the Bible says, in all your ways, acknowledge Him and He will direct your paths. The more I meditate on the word of God, the more I realize that God would rather us be good listeners. Proverbs 1:5 says, "A wise man will hear, and will increase in learning; and a man of understanding shall attain unto wise counsels." God places people in our lives that we should listen to and others that we should help guide and nurture. Everything and everyone we encounter was by design. There are things waiting for us to take ownership of in the invisible world that are incomprehensible.

In his book *The Science of Getting Rich*, Wallace D. Wattles talks about the law of perpetual transmutation. He states that energy from the formless realm or the invisible world is constantly flowing into the material world and taking form. This energy is limitless and inexhaustible. As old forms are exhausted, new forms emerge from the invisible hidden energy of the universe. Energy is always moving and transmuting into and out of form. This law of nature further tells us that energy is always in a state of motion. It will take one form, move to another form, but it's always in motion and never standing still.

This law relates our mind and our consciousness through the realization that everything seen and unseen is constantly changing. We can harness this energy and transform it into whatever form we desire. We should then realize that the energy that is with us at the moment can be focused towards good, and then the things around us and within us will change for the better. The energy is flowing into our consciousness constantly. We transform this energy into whatever we choose through our focus of attention at the moment. The formless energy is amenable to being shaped by our minds. Through learning this law, we see that change is all there is. People say, "I like things just the way they are," but they are just advertising what they do not know about this law. We must see that we are either growing or dying. We are moving forward, backward or staying the same. Everything is always changing. Do not resist change. If a person does so, then they will be going against the law and will suffer the results. Resisting change is resisting growth, and those who resist remain stagnant and prevent themselves from learning and excelling. Understand how to use this law to your benefit.

God gave us the ability to hold pictures in our minds. Visualization is a proven method that can be used to bring things from the invisible world to the physical world. Make it a priority to improve in all areas of your life so that you can easily transition with change rather than fight against it. Dream *big* and set this as your lifetime goal (page 172). Dream *big* everyday about everything in every way, and sooner or later, every thought, every action and every result will be of a huge consequence. It will become a normal thought process, and as this continues to progress, bigger and better things will be your new way of life.

Thinking small will become a thing of the past. Your energy and focus will be directed towards the bigger picture and not wasted on the small things. Everything you put your hands to will flourish as if you have the Midas touch. Your life will begin to elevate with what seems to be very little effort. But the price was paid months and years before with positive affirmations, goal-setting, action steps, vision and more importantly, faith. You believed in those things that you could not see, knowing that eventually they were going to appear in the natural.

Many of us are disappointed with the life we have because, deep down, we know that we are capable of living the life we want. We were born of creation, and innately we know that we have within us the ability to create. This is why the Bible tells us that the Spirit knows all things, because God imbued us with that knowledge. Our true self, the Spirit Man, permeates throughout our fleshly garment, engaging us to operate under our intuition and hunches so that it can direct us towards achieving our desires.

It is very difficult to have joy when you are struggling in any area of your life. To live a full, happy, abundant life, you must have and expect your desires. You were created to have a happy marriage, a joyous home life, wealth and abundance, and be in a position to teach others how to do the same. It is impossible to give to others what you do not have. You can't share wisdom if you have no wisdom. You can't help someone financially if you are poor and broke. You won't be able to show someone else how to obtain joy if it is absent from your own life. You must decide that you are going to live your life in a state of overflow so that you will have enough to pour out to someone else in need.

When God talks about abundance, He is talking about everything that makes up who we are. Most of us think of abundance as having lots of money, diamonds, gold or silver. Big houses, dream cars, fancy watches, expensive jewelry and the life that looks like that of the highest luxury. All those things are great to have, and I am not opposed to wealth by any means. What I am suggesting is that we should have an overall abundant life. Wouldn't you like to be overflowing with joy? What would life look like having an abundance of wisdom? How would you like to walk around with peace that passes all understanding? What would our lives look like if we were bursting with happiness, enthusiasm, and were fully energized? What if you had the capacity to absorb knowledge and information like a sponge? All of this is a huge part of living an abundant life. All of this is about learning to grow into higher levels of success.

You will not receive what you are not prepared for. Solomon was the wisest and wealthiest man that ever lived. According to today's monetary standards, his fortune would be equivalent to $2.2 trillion dollars. King Solomon received over $40 billion annually in gold as tribute during his forty-year reign. Looking back on the story of King Solomon, when God asked him what he wanted most, he asked for wisdom. He could not have managed such great wealth without wisdom. We will not receive what we have not grown into.

The frustration that we experience comes from knowing that we have lived half-heartedly. We were not designed to function in mediocrity. We are mortal beings created by an Almighty eternal God. Why would God create something in his own image without passing on to his creation many, if not all, of his characteristics? He has given us what no other creature on earth has, and that is the ability to control each and every thought we house in our minds.

He has given us the power of choice in every aspect of our lives. He has given us a mind to think with and to solve difficult problems. He has given us purpose. He has impregnated us with powerful imaginations. All for the sake of creating whatever world we choose for ourselves. Joy, happiness, abundance and free will are our birthrights. It is not a wish or a hope or a desire that can't be fulfilled. It is truly our destiny to have all these things, not just some of it but every single thing that brings completeness and wholeness to our lives.

Many of us end up where someone else has guided us to. Oftentimes, people are easily swayed to the thoughts, perceptions and ideologies of the majority. Usually the masses are controlled by just a handful of people who thirst for power. What is power? It is the ability to persuade the majority to serve your agenda without them really knowing it. This is why television is so critical when it comes to manipulating a large body of people.

Have you ever heard that most people believe the first story they hear or the first thing that they see? When information is dispersed to the eye gate and the ear gate simultaneously, it has a much more powerful and lasting effect. That is the very reason to use this dynamic with yourself to help you achieve what you want in life. Using the eye gate and the ear gate to go over your goals is a perfect way to let what it is that you want into the subconscious mind. Knowing and understanding the tools that God has provided us is one of the key steps to having your desires on purpose.

Doing anything with intention takes focus and persistence. Ever heard the old saying "Finish what you start"? Everything has a beginning and an ending. In order to start anything, start from the ending, and work your way back to the beginning. I know that many have heard the saying start with the end in mind. So how do you do that? You see yourself already where you want to be.

First, you should sit down and decide exactly what it is that you want. Do you want to be happy? Do you want to wake up feeling great every day? Do you want to make good money or great money? If so, exactly how much and by what time? Do you need to learn more, grow more, imagine more or dream more? Take the time necessary to figure out exactly what you want. Once you have determined exactly what it is that you want, see yourself already having it. Find yourself a pen and paper, and write a detailed description of the things you want and why. The "why" part is very important, so don't skip it. Figure out what it is that you are going to do to achieve what you have written.

If you want to be an Olympic gold medalist in figure skating and you feel as if though you have the skill set, then write it down. Write down every single goal that you want to achieve. If you want to go to France, write it down. If you want to run a marathon, write it down. If you want to be an astronaut, you must write it down. Beside each and every goal, write exactly what you are willing to do to achieve them. For instance, I want to be an astronaut and for its attainment, I will attend the Naval Academy in Annapolis, Maryland, and graduate. Once I graduate, I will serve my five years of active duty with the Navy as an ensign. When my commitment is complete, I will fill out the necessary paperwork to apply for the position of astronaut. Be as specific as possible. This will give your subconscious mind a clear picture to work with.

Take this seriously. Don't do this with half-hearted effort or a distorted view. Go all out. Thinking can be exhausting until, like anything else, you become accustomed to performing the exercise of thought. Deep thought at some point brings about revelation, and revelation will eventually create a strong desire to change. No one else can spark motivation in you. It has to be something that's developed within yourself.

Have you ever just observed a highly driven person? Michael Jordan was one of the most talented and inspiring athletes of our time. Yet, as talented as he was, he was still driven to be better. What was the motivating factor that made Michael Jordan so successful? He failed miserably. Here is a quote from Jordan.

> "I've missed more than 9,000 shots in my career. I've lost almost 300 games. Twenty-six times I've been trusted to take the game winning shot and missed. I've failed over, and over and over again in my life. And that is why I succeed."
>
> —Michael Jordan

We've heard numerous stories of people who have failed on their way to success. Michael Jordan is just one example. He was a highly competitive athlete who had a desire to win at everything he did. It didn't matter if it was a card game, baseball, basketball or the game of life. He had an insatiable desire to win. That desire is what will drive you to do the things that you have to do to achieve the life you want.

Desire ignites every fiber of your being and prompts you to act on what you know. Action propels you to move forward. Taking positive steps towards your vision can come in bite-sized pieces or huge chunks. Big achievements are easily accomplished by dissecting them one small piece at a time. Ever heard the analogy about how to eat an elephant? One bite at a time.

If you have a goal in front of you that seems insurmountable, break it up into bite-sized pieces, and then concentrate on completing that one specific piece. Diligently move from one to the other until completion. Approaching large projects this way will reduce them to manageable sizes and, with each completion, give a sense of satisfaction. Whatever you do, make a decision before you start that you are going to win. Make the attitude of winning a core part of your DNA. If you don't know how to win, learn how to win. Believe that you are a winner regardless of the circumstances you find yourself in. Have confidence that you will come out on top. To master anything, you must acquire an attitude of winning. Winners think differently, talk differently and walk differently. Confidence spews out every orifice of their being. When you are accustomed to winning, you find a way to win.

Ever watched a team that wins year in and year out? Notice the swagger that the team exhibits. It is not cockiness or pride. It is an attitude of "I know that I am the best and until you prove differently, I am thinking, talking and walking like the best."

In the 1990s, the Chicago Bulls basketball team was a dynasty. No one wanted to face them in the playoffs. Why? They were the best and everyone knew that they were, and that alone earned them respect throughout the league. They were feared. They had a swarming defense that barely allowed opponents room to breathe. They had the best offensive player in the NBA and had role players that would have been superstars on any other team. They had the attitude of winning. Here is Michael Jordan's philosophy on winning.

> "I play to win, whether during practice or a real game. And I will not let anything get in the way of me and my competitive enthusiasm to win."

> —Michael Jordan

Having that innate desire to win gives you a competitive edge. The failures that you experience in life will not shake your confidence, because winners understand that losing is part of winning. You don't become a winner by never losing. A winner learns and grows from life's losses. At some point, losses are inevitable. You will lose someone you love in death. You will lose job opportunities. Romances will come and go. Wives will leave, and husbands will depart. Unexpected illnesses and events will occur. All of these things are life, and it happens to everyone in some aspect.

Winners' lives are no different than anyone else's. The only difference is that they have learned to take a very different approach to the things that happen in their lives. Accepting the frailties as part of life better prepares you to always strive towards the results you have envisioned. You won't put your life on hold, because you have taken into account the possibility of various outcomes. No one really ever knows how they will respond when a life-changing event actually happens. The best anyone can do is identify the possibilities and hope that you handle the things you need to if and when the time comes.

One of the key components to making lasting change is to consistently do the little things. Thinking and reflecting seem like small things, and yet, it is critical to accomplishing any real change. Writing down your goals and going over them at least twice a day is a very small thing, but it pays huge dividends. Taking the time to pray about major decisions and waiting for an answer seems difficult to do on a regular basis, but it will guide you in the right direction. It is the small, simple things that get the biggest results.

> "The minute you get away from fundamentals—whether its proper technique, work ethic or mental preparation—the bottom can fall out of your game, your schoolwork, and your job, whatever you're doing."
>
> —Michael Jordan

Doing the tiny things consistently makes all the difference. Why are these simple tasks so hard for many to do? Most fail to recognize the benefits that come with doing the small things. People often take the approach that big goals require big tasks when, in reality, it's the little tasks in between that ultimately get results. Nothing of huge significance is ever done all at once. Whether building a single-family home, an apartment complex or a skyscraper, they all start with the fundamentals of building a foundation. Once the foundation is solidified, the rest of the structure is completed.

The question is, what are you willing to sacrifice to create the life that you want? Everything has a cost associated with it. Jesus gave his life on an old rugged cross to cover the sin of the world. Martin Luther King was assassinated for standing in the gap for the civil rights movement. Abraham Lincoln was assassinated because he felt that no human being should be another man's property. Of course, these were examples of the ultimate sacrifice, but you must lean into your destiny. You decide, create and then advance towards your destiny.

Everything that you do in life is signified by the effort that you are accustomed to giving. If you have developed a habit of doing very little with not much interest in performing quality work, then what you have trained yourself to do is inherently what you will do. If you have established a habit of functioning in a spirit of excellence, then everything you put your hand to will be done in the same manner.

Habits are the little things that we do each day that molds us into who we become. One of the most critical habits that we can adopt is the habit of developing our personal growth. Many of us do not take the time to evaluate or consider the value of ongoing self-development. If we don't take particular interest in our personal development, we will make a great plan, create and align our goals and work hard to achieve them, but may never come close to making them a reality.

We must grow into the level of success that we desire. You can only embrace what you have grown into. If we have not expanded our thinking broad enough to receive a million dollars, all the hard work will never get us to that level. We must first become a millionaire in our own minds before ever seeing it show up in our lives.

This is why some people continue to cycle back around time and time again. They work extra hard, they take on an added job, they start a side hustle and many become entrepreneurs, all in hopes of achieving great success. Yet, the most important work to do has not been done, so they have not grown to the level of their own expectations.

Sometimes, it is very easy to overlook the little things that make the biggest difference when our sights are already looking ahead towards an expectation that we have created but, in the creation of that expectation, we failed to develop the most key component in assuring its attainment—personal growth.

Everything hinges on how much we have developed ourselves. It may take years of reading and studying, watching videos, going to seminars and building the right relationships, but eventually, your patience and persistence will pay off. You will feel it deep down in your spirit when the time is right for you to pursue that expectation of achieving what you have envisioned and believed in.

Having instant faith is great for many, but improbable for most. Many of us have to grow our faith. There is nothing more powerful than unwavering faith. This is when you truly believe that whatever you speak will absolutely happen. Growing to that level of faith should be an ultimate goal for many of us, and yet, there seems to be an obscure understanding about faith and how it works.

Faith is more than just speaking a word that you are saying but are not believing. Faith is spoken with an understanding that you say what you believe and you believe what you say without any doubt. It is to have a clear understanding of our design and what God gave us in creation. Our words backed with unwavering faith will bring to us whatever we have said.

This is all a part of preparation to receive the things that we expect. Growing in faith and seeking personal growth—this is the work that many of us fail to do, and therefore, our expectations seem to always be just out of reach.

What are some of the things that we can do to increase our faith and ensure our personal growth? In *The 15 Invaluable Laws of Growth*, John Maxwell states that "if you are clear with what you want, the world responds with clarity" (page 4). This is a very big deal and probably the most critical. We must have a clear idea as to where we are going and why.

Sit down and make a commitment to change that right now. Do not put it off until tomorrow or wait for the right time. Make a decision this moment to get this piece completed. The longer you procrastinate on something that you can do right now, the greater the chances are that it will never get done. Make this a priority as if your life depended on it, because it does.

Put some detail behind what it is that you want: "I want to earn $500,000 a year by December 31, 2021. I will perform various duties in the form of real estate sales and home design services. I will continue to build clientele via social media and word of mouth. I will stay focused on the end result of earning $500,000 annually and be prepared for the unexpected as life happens. I will continue to gain knowledge and experience in both areas making me a valuable asset to those whom I serve, so that I can earn and receive referrals and repeat business. I will operate in excellence at all times in my relations and in my skillsets. I will set aside time each day for personal development and increasing my faith to match my level of expectation of receiving $500,000 annually."

This is an example of the type of details that get results. Don't be afraid of making mistakes during this process. Mistakes are part of the learning curve and will help grow you along the way. Learn from your mistakes, and move on quickly. Never dwell too long on a mistake that has taught you something. Decipher what you have gained from it and strive to move forward.

Place most of your energy on what you have to do as opposed to what's been done. What has been done, good or bad, has been completed and has zero relevance today, so concentrate on where you are going so that you don't get hung up on where you have been.

We all have days that we don't feel so great for whatever reason. Something happened with the kids or the job. You and your spouse had a disagreement that you haven't ironed out yet. You have a bad headache and find it hard to concentrate. You are having difficulty mustering up enough fortitude to work past what you are going through to get it done today. Things will be better tomorrow. "I will do it tomorrow. I just don't feel like it today."

So now here you are the next day—different day with a different issue. Now there is another problem that is preventing you from being able to focus on your personal growth or strengthening your faith. This is something that could potentially go on and on. What will you do to overcome?

We must find a way to do the things that we need to do even when we don't quite feel like it. Winners always make a way to complete the tasks necessary to get them to the level of their expectations. If you have big expectations, then you must have those same type of expectations for the things that you need to do on a daily basis.

Michael Jordan was a phenomenal athlete, and yet, year after year, his team would be defeated in the NBA playoffs. He lost six consecutive years from 1985 to 1990 to Milwaukee, the Boston Celtics and the Detroit Pistons. Each year, Michael Jordan was determined to get better.

He worked tirelessly on his mid-range jumpers and his assault to the basket. He worked on his defensive skills. He worked much harder in the weight room, and eventually got a strength coach. He had to get stronger, better, faster and great defensively if he was to ever get out of the Eastern Conference finals.

It took six long arduous years, but his team finally broke though in 1991 where they made their first run at an NBA championship. They defeated the Los Angeles Lakers in game five 108–101. This was Michael Jordan's first of six NBA championships.

Anyone can do the necessary things when things are always going right. The difference between those who get what they want and those who don't is the ability to work past the unexpected, uncomfortable moments that life has a tendency to drop in our laps.

Sometimes we expect things to be easier or less complicated. Truthfully, nothing worth having comes without paying a price. The biggest question we must ask ourselves is, what is the price, and are we really willing to pay it? Are we willing to put in the time and effort that it will take to match what we expect, or are we just putting some faraway wish out there hoping for a little luck in its attainment? To have the things we have never had, we must do the things that we have never done.

This may sound like a catchy phrase but, in essence, every word of it is true. This is why the formulation of habits is so valuable. Change the habit, and change the results. It's really that simple. The difficult part is reversing a mindset that's been a part of us for a very long time. The mindset that we have allowed to dominate our lives has also established the habits that we now own.

The good news is that whatever we permitted ourselves to be transformed into can be changed into whatever we decide. We are in total control of every aspect of our own condition, and changing it is just a matter of desire, persistence and a don't-quit attitude.

It is never too late to be someone different than who you are. Changing your destination in life is to have the wherewithal to be that person that you want to be in spite of who you are now. There will be naysayers, negative feedback, backstabbing and lack of support. Expect all these things, because you will experience each of them on your journey towards change. Just understand that it is part of the process of growth, and some people will be shed from your life forever. Allow yourself to be okay with the losses. It is never personal. Many of those who have known the old you can't see past what they know, so they won't be able to comprehend the level of expectations that you are shooting for.

Don't be easily discouraged for discouragement will come. Things will get sidetracked, and life's emergencies will pull you in different directions. Don't lower your expectations to support your current condition. Just continue to grow to the level of your expectation, and never ever quit until you arrive.

The decisions that you make from this point on while aiming towards your new level of expectations will determine whether you achieve what you've set your sights on or stay exactly where you are. Just because you have allowed a condition to exist, it doesn't mean that you have no other alternatives. You have the power of becoming whatever you decide to be in this very instant by seeing yourself beyond where you are now.

Don't stay committed to who you are now because it is easier to stay that way. Make a decision that you are going to be the best advocate for your own life, and drive out the fear of change so that you can develop into the person that you are capable of becoming.

CHAPTER SIX

Poverty Mindset is a Disease

An impoverished mindset is an illness. Most of us have no problem going to a physician when we are not feeling well. We have no problem popping an aspirin in our mouth when we have a headache nor swallowing down some cough syrup when we have a cold or the flu, but we do absolutely nothing towards fixing a diseased mindset. We walk around as if there's nothing wrong with our thinking. We rarely take time to nourish our minds with the Word of God or books that will help pull us out of something because it takes too much effort. A tremendous amount of energy is required to reverse an impoverished mindset.

If you never take the time to reflect on your life and start recognizing your condition, you'll remain as you are and will have no ability to grow beyond what you have become. No matter how hard you try or what steps you take before admitting to and addressing this mental disease of poverty, the cycle of scarcity will continue. One of the toughest, most draining exercises to do is honest, effective self-evaluation. Looking in the mirror and having a forthright talk about who you are and why you are where you are in life is not a task for the faint of heart. The weak will never have the courage to take a hard, deep look at their condition. It takes a lot of strength to cut through the quagmire of self-pity, fear and negative thinking. Each and every one of us know what our weaknesses are. We know where we are dropping the ball. Deep down, we clearly understand that we have a condition, but we choose not to make the necessary effort to change into what we want to be.

Most of my early years were spent in a state of poverty. My dad left my mom with seven children when I was just a young child. We were poor before my dad left us, but afterwards, we dipped even deeper into poverty. Most of my life consisted of deficiency and not having enough well into the age of adulthood. I was twenty-eight years old before I started earning enough to be considered middle class. Because I was accustomed to not having or barely getting by, I never really saw myself as having an issue. After all, this was what I knew. I didn't know anything beyond what I had been living in, which was poverty.

I remember getting out of the military at age twenty-two and moving to Tucson, Arizona, with my wife and son. We had to live in a trailer, because that is all that I could afford on $3.15 an hour. But to us, life was good, because we did not know any better. I continued to progress at the places I worked just on the basis of my natural instincts to lead. I was the oldest child of eight, so I was accustomed to being in charge of things and being thorough. My wages improved considerably over the years, but we were still living just above the poverty line.

Finally, I got a much better paying job at the copper mines, and there I met an interesting character who later became my martial arts instructor. We were talking one day after Karate practice, and he asked me if I read much. Of course, I didn't at the time, so I told him no not really. He then went to his car and brought back a book.

He looked at me and asked, "If I give you this book, will you promise to read it?"

I looked at him and smiled. "Sure, I will read it."

The book was *Think and Grow Rich* by Napoleon Hill. Needless to say, I read the book, and when I finished, I was astounded about what I had read. I had never in my life even heard of any of these concepts or principles. This sparked a desire in me to read more and more and more. I could not get enough. I read book after book after book with childlike enthusiasm.

A few years had gone by, and as I was sitting at my desk one day pondering on life and how things were going, I realized that my life had progressed dramatically financially, all because someone offered me a book that helped me see beyond poverty. I had no idea just how diseased my mindset was until I finished reading that one book. I knew that I needed to douse myself with more material like *Think and Grow Rich*. The very next read was *The Magic of*

Thinking Big by Dr. David Swartz and then *The Seven Habits of Highly Effective People* by Stephen Covey and *Unlimited Power* by Tony Robbins and on and on and on.

I had no idea as I was reading these books that my income was continuing to rise as much as it was. I was just reading and doing as each of these authors instructed. My mind was being healed from this gruesome state of poverty, but what really catapulted me to another level was when I accepted Jesus Christ as my Lord and Savior. My mind was not only healed, but renewed. Doors just started opening that I could never have imagined, and financially our lives completely changed and poverty no longer had a hold on me.

Poverty is a condition difficult to ascertain, because when you are living in the condition, recognizing that you have a diseased mind is the least of your concerns. Living in poverty only allows you to see the very next need. Looking beyond a need is almost impossible unless you associate with others who are not. Family and friends who are close to you know who you are and where you are at, and if you really want to know, just ask them. Truth is sometimes hard, but necessary if you ever want to get out of what you are in.

Since poverty is a disease, it must be cured and not just acknowledged. Knowing about something and curing are two entirely different things. If you have the flu and the doctor diagnoses you with the flu, the flu does not go away on its own. The doctor prescribes something to help you get over the flu. If you break a leg or an arm, knowing about it is great, but it has to be reset and realigned so that it can properly heal. An impoverished mindset has to be healed.

Your mind must be emptied of what has been placed there and refilled with something new; otherwise, the disease will progress and the cycle will never be broken. Poverty keeps you stuck. It's like the wheel is turning but you are not moving. You start a new business, but it never really flourishes. You get a new job and, for some reason, it never works out right. You try this and you try that, and regardless of how hard you try, nothing seems to go your way.

You may not want to hear this, but it is because of a diseased mind. No matter how hard you spin the wheel or at what speed, you end up right back in the same old spot saying all the right things but never seeing any change, because the condition causing your circumstances rests solely in a diseased mind. Heal your mind of poverty, and poverty will leave your life forever. Once poverty has been removed, restructuring how you think about money has to occur. Money is a commodity or simply a tool.

Everything we have is God's. We are just stewards in the Kingdom, placing God's money where He directs us by the unction of the Holy Spirit. Part of what keeps a person in poverty is believing what they were born into is the only option that they have. Being born into poverty does not mean that it is your birthright. Once you are born into the Kingdom of God, your birthright becomes that of the Kingdom. Just by birthright, you are immediately entered into a life of blessings and abundance. The Bible says that the old man is dead and buried and that all things become new. That includes your mindset. Romans 12:2 says, "And be not conformed to this world; but be ye transformed by the renewing of your mind, so that ye may prove what is that good, and acceptable, and perfect will of God." So what do you believe that the will of God is? Definitely not for you to live in poverty.

Poverty causes so many other negative effects in one's life. A person living in poverty rarely can see any further than their very next need. It is mentally and physically draining when the mind is steadily seeking resources to just survive. Poverty diminishes creativity. It is very hard to concentrate on creating opportunities when you can barely put food on the table or pay key bills like electricity, water and gasoline for the car.

Poverty keeps you in a constant state of worry due to shortage. You worry about being able to pay for any unforeseen events like car trouble or medical expenses. Why does a person living in poverty worry about those things? There is not enough to pay for the things they need, let alone any additional strain on the household budget. A person living in poverty usually doesn't plan for unexpected events, because they don't have the money to put back for a rainy day.

When poverty overwhelms a person's life, it puts a stranglehold on everything else. Being proactive is not an option, because they can't put aside any income to plan for something unexpected when they can barely survive the moment that they are in. Now think about that for just a minute. Many of us live a very good life unawares. Now why would I say unawares? We live in a country where food and shelter are commonplace even for the poor. We are so accustomed to having those basics that we are always looking beyond our blessings.

Years ago, when I was living in Tucson, Arizona, I went on a missionary excursion with a pastor friend of mine to Nogales, Mexico. We went into the poorest neighborhoods there. What I witnessed was absolutely horrifying. Whole families were living in small compact shelters made of nothing but cardboard. When you peeked into one of these makeshift shelters, all they had for bedding were quilts and blankets laid out all over the ground. There was no running water, no showers, no closets and no bedrooms. There was no heat or air conditioning or any other standard amenities that even some of the poorest families in this country enjoy. There were no restrooms or toilets present, no plumbing or electricity.

As poor as I was growing up, once I looked upon the living conditions of those standing before me, I realized that maybe we weren't so poor after all. I have been hungry a time or two in my life, and I have been out on the streets with no place to stay; yet, I have never been in deep poverty such as this. This was by far a different level of poor.

They would have felt like kings living in my house. We were poor according to national statistics, but we had running water, coal stoves for heat, and window fans for air, clean clothes to wear every day and a roof over our heads. We had a place that we could call home, and we felt some semblance of security even in the midst of the struggle.

We had no idea how poor we were as children because that was the only life we knew. So we were happy. We played outside until dark and skipped to school each day. We carried no burden of figuring out how to survive. That was all on our parents' shoulders. We were poor, but free. No anxiety, no responsibilities and no clue about what it took just to survive. So when I saw how they lived, there was no parallel whatsoever. This was true poverty at one of its lowest states. The living conditions were like none I had ever seen.

I not only felt remorse for the state of their condition, but when my eyes met theirs, I did not see any reflection of hope: a tired, debilitating look of despair drooped over their faces and no joy illuminating. You could absolutely feel the deep pang of poverty hovering over you like a shadow. There seemed to be no comfort mentally or physically. We went there to offer them some kind of hope by leading them towards Jesus so He could enter their hearts and fill them with joy. Jesus could heal and renew their minds even in the midst of this tragic thing called poverty. It is not normal and should never be accepted.

Many stay in poverty because it is comfortable and easy. It doesn't take much effort to live in poverty. No change is necessitated, no hard roads to travel, no inspiration to excel or improve your situation, no self-help books or positive thinking gurus to redirect your thinking. Being poor is literally one of the easiest things that one can do.

It takes effort to change a diseased mind. There must first be an acknowledgement that disease exists. Nothing can ever be cured or renewed without the recognition of an anomaly. It is not normal to live in poverty. When you accept the condition that you are in, negativity flows into your life in droves, and you become overwhelmed to the point that there seems to be no escape.

This disease was not injected overnight. It took years of negative input, poor choices, bad influences and persistent destitution to get you to this place. It is going to take some time to reverse a lifelong mindset of despair. The work must be done on your part. Until this is done, any goals, dreams or aspirations that you have will never come to fruition. The cycle will not be broken, and you will find yourself in the same old place time and time again. An impoverished mindset disrupts cognitive abilities, inhibits creativity and impedes the formulation of a clear vision for your life.

The only way to conquer this disease called poverty is to first admit that you have a condition. This is the most important step. When you can look in the mirror and the person staring back at you can say, "I have a diseased mindset and no matter how much I try to pretend that I do not, my life clearly exhibits who and what I really am," then you must ask yourself, "What price am I willing to pay for my healing? How much time, effort and resources am I willing to invest to rid myself of this disease? How can I win?" When you muster up the courage to ask the right questions, you'll get the right answers. This most likely will be one of the toughest things you will ever do in life, and it all begins with sitting down, clearing your mind and making a decision to live a healthy, abundant, harmonious life.

There are five key steps that you can take to begin the process of eliminating poverty. The first step is to start a budget. It is imperative that you know your exact income and your amount of outgo. Until you can see on paper what is coming into your household, you will invariably spend money that you don't really have. You see something that's on sale for "70% off" and it is just irresistible, but those $25 would be better suited in your gas tank or your savings account that you say you can't manage to make happen.

It takes an extreme amount of discipline to do what's right all the time; however, it is necessary if you want to defeat this thing called poverty. A budget also gives you a snapshot of money being spent unnecessarily. I had no idea how much money I was spending on frivolous things until I started doing a budget. I was in shock at the amount of money that we wasted. This money could have easily been saved or invested. The number one priority is to start a budget now! Once you establish a budget, you will begin to see opportunities to put some money away.

Saving money is always a very good idea. A person living in poverty will always think that saving money is an impossibility. It is absolutely not true. The amount of money you save is not as important as getting in the habit and developing a different mindset about money. When living in poverty, it is easy to becoming accustomed to spending every nickel that comes in. Learning to save money when money is tight teaches discipline and slowly trains your mind to see possibility. Remember, we are more concerned about making a mind shift as opposed to just saving money.

Training your mind to see money as a tool rather than a position on the wheel of economic status will gradually change your perspective about how to use it. Since money is a commodity, you must train your mind to see it as such. It is simply a promissory note used to trade for the things that we need or want in life. It is not about possession of money but access. You don't have to possess a million dollars to have access to a million dollars. Everything is a matter of perspective.

Saving money is the beginning of shifting your thinking about finances. Save just $20 a week, $10 or even $5, but save something that you do not need and will not spend. This is not money that you put back to buy something that you want later. This money will only be used if it is absolutely necessary. Your refrigerator stops working or your car needs repair would be something necessary.

Discipline yourself not to want material things that you do not need when you can't afford to buy them. Learn to distinguish the difference between a need and a want. A new outfit hanging on a mannequin that's cute is not a need. A big-screen television with all the latest functions and capabilities is not a need. Buying a new car because you are sick of the old one is not a need. Refurnishing the house because you are bored is not a need. Paying your house payments or rent, buying groceries, paying utilities and clothes to wear are needs.

Getting rid of added debt is another key step in helping to defeat poverty. A person living in poverty has no room to increase debt. Grabbing that 75″ big-screen television from Rent-A-Center for $25 a week simply because you desire it or everyone has one or you deserve it is not a good reason and is not a need. Those $25 a week would be better served in a savings account in preparation for a rainy day.

Deep down, we all do what we really want to do. We oftentimes say one thing, yet do another. We make all kinds of excuses that sound relevant to us, and we really believe that these excuses justify our irresponsibility or lack of discipline. We will say that there is no way that we can save money, not even $25 a week, but somehow the $25 were there to go rent a 75″ television from Rent-A-Center. Or we will find a way to support a hobby, but we can't find a way to put back money.

This is how you know that you are comfortable living in poverty. When you make no effort to equip yourself with the knowledge and discipline to escape this deep-rooted disease, you have succumbed to it. Family and friends can bail you out of one catastrophe after another and it will become a normal occurrence, because it is much easier for you to stay in poverty than to make the necessary effort to overcome it. The fear of upward mobility and the responsibility that comes along with having more is real.

The more you have, the more others in need expect from you. Someone else's need is not your responsibility. You always have a choice when and how much you are going to help. There is absolutely no obligation on your part to do something because you have more. Always pray to Almighty God about what you should do, and He will touch you by way of the Holy Spirit. If He doesn't prompt you to help, then God has His reasons for it. You don't have to feel any certain way about it. You shouldn't feel any guilt or shame for not helping, because you never know what God is doing in that person's life.

God knows things about this person's situation that we do not; therefore, always follow the prompting of your spirit and let God do the rest. Whatever God has prompted you to do, you do it and then it is done. Give no thoughts about it after the fact, because then you are not operating off of the prompting of the Holy Spirit but your ego.

Any time we feel that it is necessary to know the whys and why-nots of another person's condition or their journey, we are putting ourselves in God's place by assuming that we can help. God knows their entire story and He understands their journey and He alone knows what they need and why. Our only duty in anyone else's life is to provide what God has led us to provide. He is telling us what they need and exactly when they need it by prompting us to give.

Even when we are dwelling in the deepest pits of poverty, most of us are still prideful. We live a life that we want to see rather than facing the stark reality of the dilemma that we are really in. One of the main reasons that it took me so long to escape poverty wasn't because I lacked the skills or the intelligence. I was simply looking beyond my current condition to a better future that was not yet present. First, we must face the harsh reality that looking beyond our circumstance will not get us to our future without a plan and actions that will make that future a reality; otherwise, poverty will continue to rule our lives.

This is where imagination keeps us stuck. Imagination can be a great thing, or it can be a devastating problem. Like most things in life, we must always understand the sheer value in taking action. It sounds so simple, and yet, the majority of us won't do it. Imagination coupled with intent by way of planning and precise action steps will get you to those things you have envisioned.

With all that being said, how do you heal a diseased mindset and remove poverty from your life forever? You begin by having different conversations with yourself. Self-talk or autosuggestion is one of the primary tools used to start the healing process of an impoverished mindset.

Your conscious mind is the gatekeeper of your deeper level mind, the subconscious. It is the door that decides what goes in and what comes out of the most dominant mechanism for shaping who you are. Everything you've ever seen, heard, smelled, touched or tasted lives in the storehouse called the subconscious mind, and this is where the work begins to start any major transformation.

Only you can decide what nature of thought you want to allow into your subconscious mind. You will either allow thoughts of a destructive nature or a constructive nature. Both can't exist at the same time. One must live, and the other must die. Which one goes or stays is completely up to you.

The exciting thing about self-suggestion is that you have total control of what thoughts you want to feed into this powerhouse called your subconscious mind.

Think of your subconscious mind as a garden. In this garden, you can plant anything that you want. Right now, this garden is full of weeds and shrubs because it has been neglected for a long time and is in need of some clean-up to make room for the newly planted seeds to take hold and grow. How does this cleaning process begin? Self-suggestion.

Sit down and make a conscious effort to write down what it is that you desire most for your life. If it is to remove poverty from your life, then write it down. If it is to earn more money, put it to paper. Whatever it is that you want to change about your life for the better, write it down.

After writing out those things that you desire for your life, arrange each auto-suggestion into a clear, concise statement that can easily be read minimum twice a day, e.g., "I want to have a different attitude about money," or "I want to change my mindset about wealth and success." If these are a couple of things that I want to change, I would write statements similar to these.

Money is a commodity.

Money is a tool.

I live in abundance.

I have more than enough.

I deserve to be wealthy.

I am surrounded by overflow.

I am an excellent money manager.

I have plenty of money.

Money flows to me.

Money answers all matters.

Money is not a concern in my life.

Money constantly circulates into my life.

Reading these twelve powerful, concise statements every morning as soon as you wake up and every night right before you fall off to sleep will make a dramatic difference in a very short period of time. Why is this so effective? The subconscious mind is about 95 percent of our active mind and does most all the work when it comes to changing mindset and removing damaging beliefs. The conscious mind does very little compared to our subjective mind. It guards and protects what goes in and normally will prevent thoughts from getting past it to the subconscious.

The best way to get immediate change is to find a way to bypass the conscious mind and pour directly into the subconscious mind. One of the best ways to do that is to repeat over and over direct, concise statements right before falling off to sleep. Your subjective mind is always working even during sleep, and whatever you feed it right before dozing off is what it will work on while you are asleep. It is automatic and highly efficient.

All it takes is simple and diligent application to perform a complete paradigm shift from the stage that you are currently in to the life that you truly would like to live.

Victory comes to those who do the small things, which turn out to make huge changes. Persistence towards anything will produce what it is supposed to. Stick with the plan for change, and change will come.

We must decide that we are going to do what is necessary to improve our condition. The truth is, decision is what will drive everything else that you do. Once you decide to do the work that is required, you will see a significant change in your life.

CHAPTER SEVEN

Decision is the Engine That Drives Success

The most valuable component of success is decision. Life is about constantly making decisions. When do I do this or pay that? Should I go or not go? Can I afford this right now, or should I wait? We make thousands of decisions every day. So why is it so difficult for many of us to make decisions? We have plenty of practice, so what exactly is the challenge? I am sure that there are several answers to this question and you may or may not agree with the one that I propose, but when you make a decision to act, you have also made a commitment, and it is the commitment to the decision that prevents many of us from making a decision.

There are also some who are always looking to make a perfect decision and will have difficulty making decisions, or they may be fearful of making a mistake. When you make thousands of decisions a day every now and then, you are going to make a bad decision. It happens. Write it off, and move on. Making a poor decision is still a better option than not doing anything.

Making a decision puts you more in control of the outcome, whereas refusing to make a decision leaves the outcome to someone or something else. The fact is, if you don't make a decision, then you have still made a decision. Not making a decision doesn't mean that nothing is going to happen. On the contrary, something is going to happen whether you make a decision or not. It is true that, when you make a decision, it could be a bad decision, but in most cases, if you have taken the time to weigh all the information before making the decision, it will usually turn out in your favor. However, if you choose not to make a decision, oftentimes, it will end up having negative consequences.

Like anything else, a huge influx of negativity sorely impacts how you see things occurring in your life. Just like a lot of positive things create a positive environment, the result is an overflow of everything going right most of the time. When things are going well in your life, your whole demeanor changes. There is more of a pep in your step. You are more confident about the things you say and do. Everything you're involved in seems to just work no matter what it is that you lay your hands on. You look forward to making decisions, because now the fear of losing is no longer a factor. A winning attitude allows your Spirit Man to always find ways to win.

"But God hath revealed them unto us by his Spirit: for the Spirit searcheth all things, yea, the deep things of God. For what man knoweth the things of a man, save the spirit of man which is in him? Even so the things of God knoweth no man, but the Spirit of God. Now we have received, not the spirit of the world, but the spirit which is of God; that we might know the things that are freely given to us of God. Which things also we speak, not in the words which man's wisdom teacheth, but which the Holy Ghost teacheth; comparing spiritual things with spiritual. But the natural man receiveth not the things of the Spirit of God: for they are foolishness unto him: neither can he know them, because they are spiritually discerned. But he that is spiritual judgeth all things, yet he himself is judged of no man. For who hath known the mind of the Lord, that he may instruct him? But we have the mind of Christ."

—Corinthians 2:10-16

God has never expected us to rely on how the world makes decisions. He has placed in us the Holy Spirit that has the mind of Christ, which instructs and guides us in all things. God did not give us the spirit of fear, but of love and of peace and of a sound mind. So, if God has given us these things, then who is man to take them away?

Living with the disease of poverty then becomes a choice, because it is not of God. The whole idea of poverty is a deception.

Living in constant deficiency hardly leaves room for a joyful existence. How can a person be happy when all they can think about is their needs being provided? When a person lives in deficiency, seeing opportunity is almost impossible. Their minds are geared towards getting their basic needs met, let alone anything greater than that. Some opportunities only come once in a lifetime, and in order to take advantage of them, your mind must remain open and objective enough to recognize a good thing.

I am almost ashamed to admit that I have missed so many life-changing opportunities because of an impoverished mindset. As a young man, I was a sought-after artist. I had a God-given talent to draw just about anything that I saw. I had an opportunity to work with a lady who was a professional artist. My family was poor, so we could not afford to pay for her services. She was so impressed with my artistic ability that she offered to work with me for no charge. I did not take advantage of this window of opportunity, because my thinking was incorrect and I was not able to see the long-term benefit.

"Success is the continuous realization of the outcomes or results you desire."

—Herbert Harris

This lady was offering me this once-in-a-lifetime chance to dramatically enhance this God-given skill and excel as an artist. Yet, I simply could not see beyond my limited way of thinking. All I did was make every excuse possible to not have to commit to this person who was willing to give her time and expertise to help a young African American male become something more. I had blinders on because of my mindset. I was stuck in a place that I accepted as normal. It was normal for me to be in a state of deprivation. It was normal for me to live in shortage. It was normal for me not to imagine beyond my current condition. It was normal to struggle and do whatever was necessary to stay in what was comfortable.

Poverty was all I knew, and sadly it had a stronghold on me. Everything that I had heard, seen and lived up to that point led me to believe that, as a person of color, poverty was a reality of life and no matter what steps I personally took to be removed of this disparaging existence, America had already decided that I should remain poor.

I was young and very susceptible to all of the imaging that had been carefully injected into my neighborhood. I was accustomed to seeing people like me barely eating, not having enough money to pay their bills, always looking for decent work and forever hearing how much we lacked or didn't have as opposed to any kind of dreams or desires for something better.

It was almost like watching a bunch of horses with blinders keeping them from seeing what's behind or to the side of them and only seeing what was directly in front of them—which was scarcity and shortage. Everyone that I knew or had grown up with was living the exact same way that I was living, so I had no idea that something more than this existed.

For a long time, we were too poor to even own a television, so seeing people live another way was completely sheltered for us.

One day, I came home and there was a television. We would watch shows back then like "Father Knows Best" and "Leave it to Beaver" and "Dennis the Menace," but at that time, there were no shows about black people, so seeing people like me live a different lifestyle just wasn't available. And then one night while watching "The Ed Sullivan Show," this dynamic young group called the Jackson Five appeared. For the first time, I saw people of color on the television screen. It was one of the most amazing performances that I had ever seen. Watching Michael Jackson sing and dance with such joy and enthusiasm gave me a small glimmer of hope that even black people could overcome the doldrums of poverty.

I slowly began to understand that there was something about the way I was thinking that kept me in the place that I was in. I made a decision to leave Owensboro, Kentucky. By making a decision to get away from the environment that I was raised in, I became exposed to other people who looked like me doing very well in life. That's when I really got a clear perspective about the power to decide. The very first step of doing anything of any significance in life is to first make a decision to do it.

Decision is most definitely the engine that drives success. You must decide to change your circumstances, move to a new location, take on a different job or build stronger relationships. Nothing you do in life will ever happen without first making a decision. Pursuing your hopes and dreams is a decision. Acting on those hopes and dreams is a decision. Making a definite decision is what will initiate action towards your desired goals. Doing whatever it takes to do things and go places and be around people that will contribute to your personal growth is a decision.

As you began to grow, thoughts and ideas will spring at an alarming rate until the thing that you have made a decision to do manifests. Decision also brings with it confidence and the fortitude to overcome obstacles no matter how daunting they may seem. Take a runner who has decided to run and finish a marathon regardless of how long it takes. Because they have decided to not only run but finish, the end result will be a triumphant snapshot of them crossing the finish line even if they have to crawl. This alone will drive them and give them the internal strength necessary to complete the marathon. Of course, proper training also comes into play.

"Never take a break from your success journey."

—Herbert Harris

There is absolute power in decision. The better we become at decision-making and understanding what it means, the more we will accomplish. If you decide to be what it is that you want to become, then you will be what you have decided. You will live your life as that person. Your attitude, instincts, physical senses and environment will take on the new you.

There is an old saying: "Fake it until you make it." Deciding to be that which you want to become tricks our minds into a new reality. Once our inner mind has bought into the newly created you, that's all that it takes.

Have you ever been around someone who seems to have a commanding presence, and even though you can't really seem to ascertain, people flock to them and things almost always go the way they want? It is because they have mastered the art of decision-making regarding who they want to be and the things they want in life. There is no confusion, and none of it is by accident. They chose all that is happening to them by decision.

The biggest reason that most people fail is a lack of decision. In his book *Think and Grow Rich* (page 133), Napoleon Hill states, "Accurate analysis of over twenty-five thousand men and women who had experienced failure disclosed the fact that lack of decision was near the head of the list of the thirty major causes of failure. This is no mere statement of theory—it is a fact." So if this is a fact, then why don't most of us step up to the plate and make decisions? What seems to be the problem? It sounds simple enough, and yet, many have a very difficult time doing it.

One of the main enemies of decision-making is procrastination. If you want to be a good decision maker, then you must overcome putting them on the back burner. Oftentimes, waiting can make things worse. Think about some of the decisions that have transformed companies, cities and entire civilizations. What about the decision of Henry Ford to have his engineers redesign and build the V-8 engine for mass production? Although thirty-nine-year-old Frenchman Leon Levavasseur invented and patented the V-8 in 1902, Ford Motor Company perfected it.

At the time that he made this request, it was considered impossible, and yet, he knew what he wanted and refused to change his mind. His engineers would come to him month after month with little to no progress towards creating this engine. Henry Ford would listen to all of the reasons given and simply stand his ground. "Build it anyway," he would say. "Keep at it." No matter how bad the results were or how many setbacks the engineers continued to have, Henry Ford had made a decision that Ford Motor Company was going to design and build a V-8 engine that worked.

Decision will drive you past any pitfalls, stumbling blocks or bumps in the road. A clear decision means you have already reached the end goal in your mind's eye and nothing can or will deter your vision from becoming a reality.

The Bible says, "Ask and it shall be given unto you, seek and you shall find, knock and the door shall be opened." Ask with an expectation that it has manifested. Seek with a knowing that whatever you are searching for you will find. Knock believing that there is something better on the other side of the door. Don't wish for anything, but expect everything that you've hoped for. God delivers unto you the things that you have faith to receive. Never waver, and never doubt.

In the book of Mark Chapter 11 Verses 22–24, Jesus said, "Have faith in God. For verily I say unto you, That whosoever shall say unto this mountain, Be thou removed, and be thou cast into the sea; and shall not doubt in his heart, but shall believe that those things which he saith shall come to pass; he shall have whatsoever he saith. Therefore I say unto you, what things so ever ye desire, when ye pray, believe that ye receive them, and ye shall have them."

Life is a series of forks in the road, and with each one, a choice is made. Those choices, does not matter how big or how small, have a huge impact as to how our lives turn out. We also must realize that not all decisions are the same. Making a decision about what outfit to wear or what shoes match best doesn't have the same significance as a decision about where to invest money or what home to purchase. Although every decision we make matters in some way, the outcomes of some far outweigh others. Getting laughed at for wearing a bad outfit is much different than retiring broke and living on the streets.

Our egos may be affected for a short while and will mend rather quickly, but a crucial financial decision could alter our lives forever. Making decisions on a consistent basis takes a lot of discipline. We have systems in place for most things in our lives. We have financial systems, spiritual systems, personal systems and social systems, but what about a system for making decisions?

People who are successful have a process for making decisions. For one, they don't waste a lot of time on decisions that have very little impact. These are the type of decisions they kind of just play around with. Mid-range decisions are those that may affect their lives for one to two years. Moving to a different state or finishing up a degree program would be an example of some mid-level decisions. Decisions that have a much larger impact are made less often and may take more time. Deciding what house to buy in what area is a huge decision. What schools are best for our children to attend? What investments will give us the best return? These are major decisions that affect our lives now and twenty years into the future.

One of the best methods for making decisions is having clear and precise goals. Having our goals laid out can help us subconsciously make the right choices. Knowing exactly what we want in life will help guide us into making the best decisions.

If I live in New York City and I make a decision to move to San Francisco, I must first know where San Francisco is on the map. I then must make a plan to get there, whether it be by plane, train or automobile. Once the plan has been created, I must act on my plan to get to San Francisco. Setting clear-cut goals works the same way. You must first decide, make a plan and then do something. Having strategies will create a system of making good decisions more often than not. Successful people set three types of goals. There are short-range goals, which are anywhere from six months to a year. Then there are mid-range goals that span from a year to about five years, and long-range goals are from five to twenty years.

Those goals that have the largest impact get more attention, very seldom change and are made less frequently. This process works because they know exactly what they want and where to place most of their energy when making decisions. The smaller goals that have less impact can be made quickly with very little disruption to the bigger picture. Successful people always take heed to what is top priority. The long-range goals get favorable treatment, because the effect of a bad decision here could be devastating. Dissecting goals into short-range, mid-range and long-range provides steady streams of energy at the right times. This creates a constant flow of momentum towards the big picture. Each phase provides a stepping stone to the next. This type of structure makes it a lot easier to consistently make good decisions. So what happens when people using this kind of system make a bad decision? First, they take ownership for the bad decision.

Accepting responsibility allows them to take their losses and quickly move on. They have a clear path to where they are headed, so a bad decision is not their end; it is just a minor setback. They don't linger on a poor decision. Accept it, learn from it and move forward never to relive it again. It is done. They keep their goals in clear sight, and this helps alleviate the sour taste left from a bad decision. That is why it is so important that you take the time to just sit down and reflect on who you are and what it is exactly that you want in life.

Pitfalls and setbacks are part of life. Nothing ever goes as planned, so don't have an expectation that everything will go exactly as you have imagined. Something will happen much differently than how you have planned it, so be prepared to redirect as necessary. Being aware up front that things will happen that are outside of your control will prevent discouragement and help you to maintain your focus.

Always make decisions in your most ideal situations. It is never a good idea to make decisions when intoxicated, depressed, angry, emotionally distraught or mentally exhausted. If you're more alert first thing in the morning, then this might be the best time to make major decisions. If necessary, take the time you need to make a clear decision that you are less apt to change. It is better to take time to make one good decision rather than make quick decisions that change frequently. It is perfectly okay to take a day or two to make a major decision. Sleep on it, or ponder on it for a day or two so that you can be certain of what it is that you want to do.

Once you make up your mind, don't allow yourself to be easily influenced to change it. When you allow outside influences to change your direction, resentment will take hold. Lingering resentment will affect future decisions and the stability of a once-clear path no longer exists. This inevitably affects your confidence, and now you begin to second-guess whatever decision you make from that point forward. Trust in what you have decided for your life, and believe in yourself enough to stay the course.

When making decisions, start with the end result in mind. Make every goal from short-term to long-term a stepping stone towards that end result. Set reasonable goals. Unrealistic goals can cause disappointment and even anxiety because of the feeling that you have failed or fallen short. This is why it is so important to understand the strategies used to achieve big-time goals. Remember short-range, mid-range and long-range goals help you achieve a sense of balance towards the larger, more important goals. This will prevent burnout, and the mini steps of the short-range and mid-range goals will always advance you closer, with each advancement giving you a series of small victories to celebrate. Every victory towards a much greater achievement is paramount to any major success.

Another key component to learning to make and stick to decisions is keeping major decisions about the direction of your life to yourself, or if you do share them, make sure that it is shared with those who not only support where you are going, but will help in any way possible. Only choose those who will help you maintain focus and complete harmony as you strive towards your major goals. Remember, many people are not standing for your success, but eagerly waiting for your demise.

This is not necessarily intentional. Most people are well-meaning, and some really believe that their opinions are adding value. Know that many that you come into contact with are battling with fears and insecurities that they have not yet recognized or come to terms with. All they know to share is the level of what they have been educated to, which may not be enough to assist you on your journey.

Most people have an opinion and many of those opinions are based on something they have heard or seen but not personally experienced, so they really aren't qualified to talk to you about an outcome that they have never realized in their own life. Conjecture is their made-up reality that they are attempting to pass on to you as fact. This is why the goals you make should be well guarded until you achieve them.

There will be plenty enough obstacles without the added intervention of unwarranted opinions. If you are in need of advice or factual information, gather it without exposing your reason for needing it. Most people want to feel a sense of value or importance, and their opinions reflect what they can't see themselves doing rather than seeing the capabilities of what you can do. Spend time with yourself and understand who you are and what drives you. If you are of a healthy mind and you have decided your own path in life, don't ask too many people outside yourself about what needs to be done to accomplish what you've set out to do.

Don't be afraid to sit down and exercise the art of thinking. You would be absolutely surprised at how many of those who you trust as supporters are silently envious of who you are and will do anything to derail your dreams. To prevent yourself from having to fight silent battles, it is better to let the world see what you're doing as opposed to telling them what you are doing. Learn to associate with those who are like-minded. Train yourself to act on what you have decided.

Making a decision is only the first step to realizing a dream. The wheel of action is what will bring it into realization. The action to pursue a decision you have made comes with a certain amount of risks.

President Abraham Lincoln made a decision that inevitably cost him his life. On January 1, 1863, Lincoln signed the Emancipation of Proclamation Act, which started the process to dissolve the long-standing institution of slavery. Lincoln understood the consequences of his decision, yet he overcame his personal struggles and fears to do the right thing. Many died on the battlefield to uphold the president's decision. Lincoln's decision took a lot of courage. He lost friends, associates and many of his supporters. More lives were lost in the Civil War than any other war in history. This was no easy decision, but it was the best decision. Some decisions that you make will test your mettle and causes you to lose sleep at night, but it doesn't mean that it was the wrong decision. Sometimes, the toughest decisions turn out to be the best decisions.

Probably one of the greatest decisions ever made was the signing of the Declaration of Independence—a document signed by fifty-six men who knew that there were only a possibility of one of two outcomes, the freedom of a nation or the death of each and every one of them. This is another great and memorable event in history where one decision dramatically changed the course of an entire nation. The bigger the risk, greater is the decision. No major decision that influences dramatic change or development comes without risks.

Think about the decision of General George Washington to burn the ships on the banks of the Delaware River to prevent British troops from pursuing his depleted army. What else did this decision do? It let every single soldier witnessing this event know that there was no way to return unless they were victorious. The one avenue for any type of retreat had been swiftly removed with ships burning and sinking behind them as they marched forward to either conquer or die.

Now imagine the finality of this one decision. It is Christmas night, and they are already battling extreme and unpredictable elements. The Delaware River at their crossing point was partially frozen. Freezing rain had begun to fall as treacherous winds cut through each soldier, chilling them right down to the bone. The freezing rain turned to snowfall as it gently illuminated the blackness of the night. Cold, wet, hungry and exhausted—it didn't matter to any of these men. They had laser-like focus to complete the mission regardless of the conditions.

George made that decision because it was their last hope of snatching victory. They had already succumbed to several unexpected defeats prior to that brutally cold night. It took courage to look death straight in the eye and defy every ounce of its existence with one valiant ultimatum in mind: victory or death. Life's decisions end up transforming you, and where you end up heavily depends on how well you've made decisions.

We are bound by the decisions we make and driven by the outcomes they have committed us to. Decisions are very powerful. They give us a means to an end towards something that we now believe we can achieve. Once hope is stirred by simply making a sound decision, anything is possible.

CHAPTER EIGHT

You Are What You Act Like

Be what you desire to become, and it has to manifest. Romans 4:17 says, "Call those things that be not as thou they were." God was talking to Abraham about faith and believing the promise that he was the father of many nations and that his seed would come from his loins in spite of his old age. Abraham, being a man of strong faith, believed that God was able to deliver what He had promised.

When God tells us to believe it already exists without ever physically seeing the manifestation, He is clearly letting us know that it is your faith alone that will bring it forth.

I will never ever forget a sermon given by Pastor Bill Winston about faith being the currency of Heaven. He was preaching at our church and as usual brought a Word specifically for me. That alone made me realize why we can't please God without faith. God has instilled in us all a knowing of his existence without ever having to see Him. All we have to do is look around, and you can see God at every turn starting with our very own design.

The human body is by far the most intricately designed machine that we have ever seen. It is an amazing creation all by itself, let alone the supporting evidence shown around the planet. God expects us to believe what He has said. It is impossible for God to lie. When God is telling us to go ahead and believe that we have received something before we actually see material evidence, it is because He knows what He created in us and for us.

There is an old saying that many of us have heard at some point in our lives: "Whatever the mind can conceive and believe, it can achieve." When we break this down into segments, we must start with what the mind is. What exactly are we talking about when we say what the mind can conceive?

I believe that the mind is your eye or your vision. The Bible says that God gives us the desires of our heart. With that being the case, God places in you a vision. That vision is etched into your mind, which then becomes a burning desire, and this desire is what fuels you to action. The actions ignited by that desire will transform you into what you need to become, and that will bring about manifestation.

I know that this all may sound a bit confusing, but it truly works. Have you ever just sat someplace where children were play-ing and observed them? There is so much to be learned from a child. There are no restrictions in their thinking. Their imagination runs rampant, and it expresses itself as different characters and is presented to new worlds.

Kids actually believe everything that they are saying and doing without any doubt. Whatever role they adapt during play time is a real and serious transition from who they currently are to that person that they want to be. Ever asked them who they are when all of this is going on? They will blurt out with the utmost sincerity and enthusiasm, without hesitation, "Can't you see that I am Batman?" They'll jump in their makeshift Batmobile and make noises as if they really are in one. They'll jump out of the Batmobile and mimic the character Batman right down to the flowing black cape. At that very moment, without a doubt, they are Batman, and you'll never convince them otherwise. They are exactly who they imagine themselves to be. They have wholeheartedly transformed into that character.

This works for children because they have not been subjected to any kind of restrictions in their thinking. No one has yet told them that they can't do so; they just function on their internal instincts to do and become whatever they have imagined.

There have been many great and successful persons who have clearly lectured on the power of imagination. A man by the name of Neville Goddard was one of the pioneers teaching on the subject of imagining what you wanted to be or do and without a doubt it coming into manifestation.

He once told a story of a young man who imagined himself owning a business in a large building. This young man imagined it all the time, and one day, unexpectedly, he bumped into a man who happened to have a lot of money. This man saw something in him and decided to invest in him.

The young man had been staring at a large empty building, and as he stood there imagining his business successfully up and running in that very building, a man happened to come by that same spot and struck up a conversation with him. As they talked, the rich man offered to buy the young man the building. Even though the young man had not a penny to contribute nor any way to repay him, the rich man saw something in him that he trusted and offered a solution.

He came up with the idea of having the young man pay him back annually an additional 6 percent above the principal for ten years. This type of agreement required no money and no collateral, but it did give the young man ownership of the building. Now that the young man owned a building, he could start the business that he had always envisioned.

Imagine all he had was a dream. He had no way of knowing how it all was going to materialize, but he had constantly seen every detail in his imagination. He was living as the business owner that he had been imagining, and the law of attraction did exactly what it was supposed to. It provided a way when there seemed to be no way.

Oftentimes, we fix our thoughts on something without an understanding of what is occurring. Whether it be something positive or negative, we bring into our lives what we think about all day long. Acting as if you already have what you are hoping for draws it to you at an alarming rate.

Ever wondered why great actors are so good at what they do? They can imagine themselves to be whoever they decide by using their very skillful imagination. They have to believe they are actually the character they are portraying in the movie that they are acting in.

When we were small children, we had no problem pretending to be someone or something else. We were Superman, Batman, the Lone Ranger, but whoever we decided to become, we became. No hesitation and we could care less what anyone else thought about it. Now fast-forward to the present. If it worked then, why wouldn't it work now? What happened in our lives that took us away from imagining? People started pushing their fears and beliefs off on us. Negative programming was everywhere: "You can't do this," or "You can't do that." "That's crazy," or "That's not normal," or how about "No one else does that, so why are you?"

You get laughed at, ridiculed or just plain embarrassed by others who really don't understand what it is that you are trying to accomplish. Just because everyone else believes that you are unorthodox or not normal doesn't mean that it's right. It simply means that you are coming from a place that they can't see themselves operating from. That's okay. Creativity can look strange sometimes.

A person who is focused on becoming what it is that they see in their mind can sometimes appear to be off center, but who makes the rules? Who determines what is normal and what is not?

Society usually places stipulations on a few on the basis of the overall beliefs of the whole. Our fellow citizens who believe in a majority view usually persuade those outside of that to conform by social manipulation.

If you do not fall in line with what the majority believes, they may make fun of you, or you may be deemed unstable, be ostracized or alienated. In any case, that magnificent imagination slowly disappears. The stronger need for approval takes over, and sooner or later, you end up complying with the rules that society has adopted.

You find yourself buying into the story of growing up, getting a good education so you can be hired at a great company, save money in your 401K and retire. Your imagination now becomes stagnant and no longer has any reason to display itself. Imagining to be something greater or something different than the ordinary no longer seems to be a part of who you are; therefore, the drudgery of everyday ordinary life takes hold, and you become just another rat in the maze of big corporations.

That is why Jesus emphasized to become as that little child, because children in their innocence and power of imagination know how to become what it is that they want to be without a care in the world about society's rules. "Call those things that be not as though they were" is one of my favorite Bible verses, and the significance of those few words can transform dreams into reality expeditiously.

I have been in situations where I was all alone. During those times, reflecting on my life allowed me to clearly understand the significance of being a thinker. Being a thinker can mean many things to many people, but for me, it means to constantly evaluate who I am, where I am with respect to self-growth and what it is that I should be doing to bring to life what is in my imagination.

Thinking is free of charge. It pays huge dividends, and you don't need anyone's permission or acceptance to do it. The benefits of deep thinking far outweigh the time and energy it takes to formulate the habit. Like anything, the more you do it, the better you become. As you become more proficient, you will also learn to be blatantly honest about the role you have played in shaping your own life.

You will develop a deeper connection with your spiritual person, and fears will begin to drop off. As your fears grow wings and take flight, as your mental limitations begin to shrink and become so small that they no longer matter, you will begin to challenge your limits. Confidence begins to soar, and you become absolutely fearless. As you take on new endeavors, you no longer question whether you can do it; your only thought process is how you can get it done.

Thinking on a consistent basis makes you come face to face with your real self. The Spirit Man that God breathed from his own nostrils to give life, our earthly dressing called our body is what connects us to earthly components. Thinking takes us far beyond what the body can offer. Thinking is what makes us unique to all the other animals on God's green earth.

God has given us the ability to self-assess and grow into whatever it is that we want to become. Notice that I said "grow into whatever it is that we want to become." Now I realize that this sounds slightly different than what we have heard in times past; however, you can never become what you have not grown yourself into.

I can say everyday several times a day that I am a millionaire. If I am just saying that I am a millionaire, but I have not resolved in my mind that I am a millionaire, I will not become a millionaire. Faith of being must be apparent before becoming.

Let's take a look of one of the most talented boxers of all time: Muhammad Ali. He was not only talented, but he believed something about himself that propelled him to a whole different level than any other heavyweight fighter. On October 30, 1974, Muhammad Ali was a huge underdog against the all-powerful George Forman. Ali was thirty-two years old, whereas George Foreman was only twenty-five. George Foreman's record was 40–0 with 37 knockouts. The only person that believed that Ali was going to win was Ali himself. He believed himself to be the greatest. He spoke it, he walked it and he lived it. He portrayed himself as the greatest in every area of his life. George Foreman was about to risk everything to defeat a legend. After all, wasn't Ali much older? Considered over the hill in the sports arena? George Foreman was young, strong and confident, but he was faced with something that he was not familiar with. He was facing a man who truly believed that he was the greatest, and in Ali's mind, no matter the foe, he had already won before he ever stepped foot in the ring that night.

There is an old saying that winners win and losers lose. Despite George Foreman's immaculate record, he had never faced the power of unshakable, unyielding, immutable faith like that of Muhammad Ali. Ali had experienced a similar scenario back on February 25, 1964, against the formidable Sonny Liston. He was a 7–1 underdog in that fight.

He ended up shocking the entire world with a seventh-round technical knockout. Ten years later, it was the same situation with a different opponent. The odds on this fight pegged Ali as a 4–1 underdog. But the mind of Ali had been walking, talking and living like the greatest his entire boxing career, and George Foreman was about to embark on what it felt like to face a legend.

It took eight rounds for the greatest to rise up to his legendary status. For most of those rounds, George Foreman appeared to be punishing Ali blasting his ribs and midsection with thunderous blows. Ali, with a brilliant plan of attack, allowed Foreman to expend all his energy, and when he had nothing left, Ali rose up and dazzled George with a barrage of pinpointed, laser-like blows that sent him crashing to the canvas lifeless. There he lay defeated and in total shock of the outcome.

From the time that Ali began his professional boxing career, he acted like what he had been saying all along, that he was the greatest. Ali always spoke like what he wanted to be. "Float like a butterfly and sting like a bee; rumble, young man, rumble" has been etched into my mind from that very first day I heard it explode from his mouth with such conviction and enthusiasm. From that day, I admired him and followed his career expecting him to be exactly what he said.

The most rudimentary element of huge success is garnered with an unshakable belief in oneself. Never deny yourself an opportunity to plant good seeds into the fertile ground of your mind. Whatever you plant there will eventually show up in your life. It all begins from within before it ever shows up without.

You have to plan for your personal growth. John Maxwell gave an example of a very profound statement by Bruce Springsteen in his book entitled *The 15 Invaluable Laws of Growth* (page 3): "A time comes when you need to stop waiting for the man you want to become and start being the man you want to be." Growth is not an accident.

The best way to improve the world around you is to first improve yourself. I once read that the world will step aside for the man who knows where he is going. Once you know exactly what it is that you want in life, then take on the habit of action. If you want to work out, get up and go to the gym. Showing up is the magic behind winning the battle regardless of what it is.

If you want to be a playwright, then sit down and write. If you want to be a chef, start by cooking whatever it is that you can cook. Just start. Lay your dreams before you in the form of writing them down. Make long-term and short-term goals that take you towards your dreams. Then act on what you have imagined.

It all sounds very simple, and yet, most people will never do what they dream. It will remain hidden in the crevices of their mind never coming to fruition simply because of inaction. We must learn the power of motion. Stagnation can't exist if you are moving towards the things you seek. Believe it or not, motivation doesn't come to you by the waving of a magic wand. No one can pray it on you. Telling yourself a thousand times to get up off the couch won't do it. The only thing that will bring about motivation is learning the art of doing. Whatever it is that you want to do in life, just get up and do it.

Remember the Nike commercials years ago whose main selling point was "Just Do It!"? The reality is that, until you get in the habit of acting on what it is that you desire, it will never happen. No matter what it is that you want to accomplish, there must be some intentionality. Having a vision won't be any more than a dreamer's dream without action.

If you don't move it from the corridors of your mind to paper, and put action steps for its achievement, it will most likely be carried to the grave right along with your corpse. Once you are dead and buried, your dream no longer has life, and the realization of one day making a difference is hidden beneath dirt and rubble never to rise again.

There are many great inventions lost to the grave—best-selling books, scientific breakthroughs, master generals and world leaders that were but never became, simply because they held a dream that they failed to act on.

Don't take a chance on that marvelous idea never being heard or that new design never getting a chance to add value to society. Make yourself adept at taking action. There is an old saying: "Never put off for tomorrow what you can do today."

Most lasting ideas come in the middle of the night when in deep sleep. How many times have you been awakened in the wee hours of the morning with an idea? You think, *Wow! That's a great idea.* You fall back off to sleep believing that you'll wake up the next morning and remember that marvelous idea that woke you up. You exert every ounce of thought trying to recall that idea, but regardless of how hard you concentrate, it doesn't come.

Intentionality means taking a proactive approach. Get a notepad and pencil and put on your night stand, and when you are awakened in the middle of the night with an idea, grab that pencil and write it down right then and there in that notepad. When you wake up the next morning and look, you will be amazed at what is written there. Now all you have to do is devise a plan to make it a reality. See the end product in your mind, and work from there. Begin with the end in mind, and work backwards to create your goals and action plans until that end picture becomes a reality.

This seems a very simple process, yet most people never take the time to actually do it. Remember, you are what you act like. People who achieve great things don't do it by accident. They create what they create with intentionality, and it does not matter who you are or what your background is, this method holds true.

Change your thoughts, master your words, believe what you have envisioned and create a brand-new life. It works for people with very little money or people who have a lot of money. It has nothing to do with your financial position or societal standing; it has everything to do with what you think, say and believe. Ideas, words and faith—it is the most powerful combination known to man. People throughout time have changed nations with this proven formula.

Jesus Christ had a huge impact on the world preaching the gospel. His thoughts, words and beliefs transformed millions, and continue to this day. No other person has changed the worldview the way Jesus has.

Mahatma Gandhi led a peaceful revolt to gain civil rights of Indians who were harshly discriminated against by white British authorities. After witnessing such deep-seeded hatred, Gandhi decided to commit his life to eradicating the disease of prejudice, while enduring hardships and persecutions along the way. Like Jesus, Gandhi was eventually murdered. A Hindu extremist was terribly upset over Gandhi's tolerance of Muslims and shot him to death January 30, 1948. Gandhi was seventy-eight years old when he was assassinated.

The fifties and sixties were very turbulent times in America. The Civil Rights movement was steam-rolling across this great nation, and one of the greatest black leaders emerged to take on what seemed to be an insurmountable challenge for change.

Martin Luther King Jr. was recognized as one of the most impactful and cherished leaders during the twentieth century. He played a crucial role in dissolving the legal segregation of African American citizens in the United States. He also played a huge role in the enactment of the Civil Rights Act of 1964 followed by the Voting Rights Act of 1965. Both of these bills were instrumental in allowing blacks to justifiably participate in citizenry rights as well as the political system.

Martin Luther King Jr. won the Nobel Peace Prize in 1964, and he will always be remembered as one of the most influential and inspirational black leaders of our time. These men saw harsh and unfair circumstances in the lives of other human beings, and rather than stand on the sidelines and become a part of the majority, they all stood up and became a majority of one.

They led those without hope out of a disparaging situation and elevated them to places of freedom and equality. They didn't hope to lead nor did they wish to lead; they just decided to lead, and from that moment, they simply led.

In an instant, we can become everything that we hope to be. It's all a matter of thinking and believing. When you take a long, hard look at the person in the mirror, the person looking back at you must see value. You will never make an effort to develop anything that you don't see value in.

Michael Jordan is considered among the greatest basketball players of all time. He had tremendous talent and developed skills that surpassed most of those he played with. What made him so great at this game called basketball?

First of all, he was very committed to both mental and physical development. In order to be the best player in the world, you must train like the best player in the world. Jordan trained five hours a day six days a week. He had two shooting sessions a day and took five hundred shots per session, i.e., six thousand shots per week.

He did strength training so that he could endure the physicality when driving down the lane. He worked his way up to lifting 225 lbs. overhead shoulder presses. He did squats on a balance board to help improve agility.

He wanted to be a champion and wanted to work harder than anyone else, so he did. To become a champion, he had to first see himself as a champion. That was what drove him to work as hard as he did. We must be able to see our self-worth. This is what will drive us to do the impossible, the unthinkable and the unfathomable.

By becoming what it is that we see, we can overcome the harshest obstacles. We can conquer exhaustion and mental fatigue. What others find difficult to achieve, becomes easy to those who see their real worth.

CHAPTER NINE

Have Your Desires on Purpose

You can have everything you desire in life on purpose. How many people do you personally know who believe that they can have anything they want? Being able to get whatever you want in life can be very gratifying. There are still problems that surface and unexpected circumstances that are not pleasant, yet, those who know how to get what they want and know where they are headed tend to handle the pitfalls of life more effectively.

They are constantly working towards a predetermined target. The big picture stays present in their minds, and the issues of life never pulls them off track. When you have a burning desire to see a thing to completion, obstacles don't have the same relevance or any power over your destiny.

Knowing exactly what you want in life is the start of getting everything you desire on purpose. Like anything worth having, you will have to sit down and invest some time and thought into the things you want.

Our subconscious mind operates a lot better when it has something to work towards. You don't plant apple seeds to get oranges; you plant orange seeds to grow oranges. A misdirected mind has no idea what it is that you are aiming for. If you have not given it instructions for the things that you desire, you will get what you get.

NASA doesn't just launch a space ship into orbit without precise calculations and directions on how to get to where it is going. The captain of a cruise ship doesn't leave the bay without knowing the destination. Your subconscious mind is bound to the things you have told it to do, and without precise instructions, it is impossible for it to help manifest what you want in life.

If you want a maroon-colored Mercedes Benz with cream interior leather seats, a solid oak dashboard, brown in color, all electric, fully loaded with 80,000-mile Michelin radials and a sunroof top with less than 500 miles on it, then say exactly that. The better the description, the greater chance that you'll get precisely what you presented.

If you desire to weigh 165 lbs. of lean muscle with 12 percent body fat and radiant smooth skin, then pass that information along to your subconscious mind and it will do everything possible to give you what you have asked for. Scripture is very clear about this. Ask, and it shall be given you. It doesn't say that *maybe* it will be given you or it *could* be given you. It plainly says that it *shall* be given you.

Now if God said that it shall, then believe that it will. That is the very first step in having our desires on purpose. God designed a world that would take care of His creation, and with this world, He provided tools that work incessantly to help us get whatever we want. By describing precisely what we want, the laws that God put in place start working on our behalf. There are specific laws that were designed for our sole benefit.

Earlier we spoke of the law of gravity. We also touched on the law of attraction, but there are a lot of other laws that are always working invisibly. Every thought is a form of energy, and that energy operates under key components. There are several laws we rarely hear about that help with the manifestation of the things we desire.

There is the law of confession, the law of recognition, the law of excellence and the law of favor. Again, like many other laws, these all work in conjunction to bring things from the vast invisible world to the physical world.

God created all things, and all things are created by God. The Bible says that "for by him were all things created, that are in heaven, and that are in earth, visible and invisible, whether they be thrones, or dominions, or principalities, or powers, all things were created by, and for him."

I want to reiterate this point that God created these laws and they are not separate from His creation. Some identify these laws as universal laws and seem to believe that they are something separate.

They are simply perceived to be separate, yet they are one and the same.

God created the universe, so every law functions as God designed. The law of gravity is a universal law just as the law of relativity is. God knew when He formed the Heaven and the earth that He had to put eternal systems in place to assist His eternal creation.

Keep in mind that man was created to live out eternity. There are both spiritual and physical laws, and one works in the invisible realm while the other works in the physical. Everything produced in the physical must first be drawn from the invisible.

Everything God created has atoms and molecules, which then create matter, and that is simply the solid form. The words we speak are vibrational, and that helps us maintain a certain frequency. Positive frequencies are higher than negative frequencies. Every word that comes out of your mouth has a frequency attached to it, and it will bring exactly what it is designed to.

That is why God emphasizes how powerful the tongue is, because we constantly produce words. Words are energy, and energy attracts like energy. These are all designed laws, and we don't have to accept them for them to work. Gravity could care less whether you believe that it works or not; it is going to do what it was designed to do. Every law has its purpose, and they will always work the way they were designed.

God knew exactly what He was doing when He created the worlds, suns and stars. These laws work without effort. That is why the Bible says God is not mocked because you absolutely get what you give whether it be in deed, word or thought. Everything you think, say and do has with it a price. Do not be deceived: "God is not mocked, for whatsoever a man soweth, that shall he also reap."

The law of confession ensures that this will always hold true. You sow with your words, and those words attract like vibrations, which then materialize in your life. There is no escaping what you say. Your life will always indicate what your words have created. Learning the power and value of our words is one of the most important lessons of life.

This is why lawyers exist. They are masters of words and word manipulation. People are held to what they have said throughout history. When kings ruled the world, the very words spoken from their lips were law. Once a decree was made by a king, it stood no matter what.

Job 22:28 KJV says that "we shall also DECREE a thing and it SHALL be ESTABLISHED unto us." We must believe that we will have what we say. We are designated kings here on earth by Jesus who is the king of kings, in other words, us. So if we are kings and we decree a thing, then we must know that it will come to pass. By our own words, we can have everything we desire *on purpose*.

We should expect what we say has already taken place and will manifest without doubt. The moment we speak anything in belief, it is already done and is moving towards us. If it did not surface the very instant you spoke it, then just give it time, because it has been transferred from the invisible to the visible and will soon be in your possession.

It is faith that is the substance of things hoped for and the evidence of things not seen. What is substance? According to the dictionary, substance is "matter of which a thing consists, physical matter or material, a species of matter of definite chemical composition, the subject matter of thought, discourse, study, etc., the actual matter of a thing, as opposed to the appearance or shadow, reality." So when the Bible says in Hebrews 11:1, "Now Faith is the substance of things hoped for and the evidence of things not seen," it's telling us that the currency of faith will manifest the things we hope for from the invisible world to the natural world.

Faith is knowing and expecting a thing without physically seeing it. God shows us our future through visions and dreams just like He always has. In Acts Chapter 9:10-12, the Bible says, "And there was a certain disciple at Damascus, named Ananias; and to him said the Lord in a vision, Ananias. And he said, Behold, I am here, Lord. And the Lord said unto him, Arise, and go into the street which is called Straight, and enquire in the house of Judas for one called Saul, of Tarsus: for, behold, he prayeth. And hath seen in a vision a man named Ananias coming in, and putting his hand on him, that he might receive his sight."

Another illustration of this is in the book of Genesis Chapter 15 Verse 1: "After these things the word of the LORD came unto Abram in a vision, saying, Fear not, Abram: I am thy shield, and thy exceeding great reward." Many are familiar with the story of

Joseph and the dream that he shared with his brothers. In Genesis Chapter 37:5-11, the Bible says, "And Joseph dreamed a dream, and he told it his brethren: and they hated him yet the more. And he said unto them, Hear, I pray you, this dream which I have dreamed: For, behold, we were binding sheaves in the field, and, lo, my sheaf arose, and also stood upright; and, behold, your sheaves stood round about, and made obeisance to my sheaf. And his brethren said to him, 'Shalt thou indeed reign over us? Or shalt thou indeed have dominion over us?' And they hated him yet the more for his dreams, and for his words. And he dreamed yet another dream, and told it his brethren, and said, 'Behold, I have dreamed a dream more; and, behold, the sun and the moon and the eleven stars made obeisance to me.' And he told it to his father, and to his brethren: and his father rebuked him, and said unto him, 'What is this dream that thou hast dreamed? Shall I and thy mother and thy brethren indeed come to bow down ourselves to thee to the earth?' And his brethren envied him; but his father observed the saying."

God is the same today as He was yesterday. He does not change. He still communicates with us the same way that He did in the day of Joseph. Even though God still speaks to us this way, many modern-day Christians are not sensitive enough in the spirit to recognize a vision or dream from God and many blessings are simply bypassed.

Hearing from God means spending time with Him and getting to know who He is and how He operates. A great start is reading the

Word of God and praying for discernment. In doing so, the hidden things of God will be revealed to us.

Daniel Chapter 2:22 tells us that "He revealeth the deep and secret things: he knoweth what *is* in the darkness, and the light dwelleth with him." God has put everything in place to make sure that we have our desires on purpose. He left nothing out. He gave us the power to create by the words we speak with faith. He gave us laws that work in our favor if we just learn what they are and how to use them.

He gives us visions and dreams for us to spiritually interpret showing us our future. Since we are spirit housed in a body, we should be more in tune with the spiritual realm than the physical world. God is Spirit, and He breathed into man made from the dust of the ground the breath of life. Now that being said, everything we desire starts from the spiritual realm and is then manifested into the physical world.

What starts this process? We are shown our future in a vision or a dream given to us by God. This creates in us a burning desire. We begin thinking about this future day and night. Whatever we think about all day long is what we become. Now this vision has become surreal in our minds, and we begin to speak what is inside of us. Once we start speaking by faith what is inside us, it is created right then and there in the spiritual realm and has no choice but to manifest into our physical reality. It is a done deal, and all we have to do is look for our stuff because it is coming just as sure as the sun rises.

God tells us that "death and life are in the power of the tongue: and they that love it shall eat the fruit thereof another verse says that whatever you ask in prayer, you will receive, if you have faith." God provides verse after verse ensuring that we will get what we say. This is one of my favorites: (Mark 11:23) "Truly, I say to you, whoever says to this mountain, 'Be taken up and thrown into the sea,' and does not doubt in his heart, but believes that what he says will come to pass, it will be done for him."

Having what we say on purpose has been already thought of, and systems were created by God to make sure of our success. The verse "Ask and it shall be given you, seek and ye shall find, knock and the door shall be opened" takes on a very different perspective once we clearly understand the creative power of our words coupled with belief. Isaiah 55:11 is a perfect verse for this discussion. "So shall my word be that goeth forth out of my mouth: it shall not return unto me void, but it shall accomplish that which I please, and it shall prosper in the thing whereto I sent it." I get goose bumps reading this verse, the thought that nothing God says "returns unto him void and he created us in his image which means that our words will not return unto us void."

This is why God says that we will be judged by every idle word we speak, because our words mean something and words of idleness have absolutely no purpose. God speaks with purpose, and He doesn't say anything unless it is working for good. In order to use a tool, you must first know that the tool exists, and then you must learn what the tool's function is and how to use it. Knowing the systems that God has put in place is where asking, seeking and knocking comes in. Ask for wisdom, and God will give it liberally. Seek understanding, and it will be provided. Knock on doors of opportunity, and they will be opened.

King Solomon asked for wisdom on how to fairly judge his people, and what did God do? He not only gave him wisdom, but also riches beyond measure. It is difficult to have a life on purpose if you don't know that you can. God's Word says that "wisdom is the principal thing; therefore get wisdom: and with all thy getting get understanding." This is why it is important to continue to grow yourself.

Investing in ourselves broadens our view of the world and those around us. When we eliminate dirt and filth from our own lenses, we can see clearly to help grow those around us. Understanding who you are and how you function will always be a benefit to the Kingdom of God. When you think like a king, walk like a king and take on the persona of a king, then every word out of your mouth will produce the very thing you have spoken.

God has given us all the instructions on how to get everything that we want. So there it is. We think on the vison that God has placed in us, we speak what comes out of our heart, but there is one more critical piece that will help reinforce what we think and what we speak. Write down the vision. Take whatever thoughts are housed in your mind and put them on paper. No matter how scattered and unorganized they seem to be, just get your thoughts emptied onto a piece paper.

God says, "And the LORD answered me, and said, 'Write the vision, and make *it* plain upon tables, that he may run that readeth it.' For the vision *is* yet for an appointed time, but at the end it shall speak, and not lie: though it tarry, wait for it; because it will surely come, it will not tarry."

Writing things out on paper has so many benefits, but I am only going to share a couple. Seeing your vision on paper makes it more real. It is no longer just swirling around in your mind as a mere thought or pipe dream. Now it is on paper, and you have written it with your own hands. This triggers something in your subconscious mind that causes it to act. Once you have written something down, your mind commits to what has been written.

Have you ever written down a list of errands and for some reason lost the list? So you run around seemingly erratically with no direction. You go to this place and to this store, and then you run across town and, before you know it, the end of the day is upon you and you're headed home. You get to the house and come across the list that you had earlier misplaced. To your surprise, you actually completed everything on the list without having it. How did you remember to do everything on that list with no list? When you actually wrote that list on paper, it was ingrained into your subconscious mind. Our subconscious mind remembers everything that we have ever smelled, touched, tasted, heard or seen. So when the list was actually written to a piece of paper, two things happened. It was written and it was seen, and if you repeated the list out loud, then it was also spoken. This reinforced what the subconscious mind knew had to be completed, and it stored a snapshot of that list never to be lost or forgotten.

It knew exactly what was on the list, and because there was no pressure or much thought once the list was presumed lost, the subconscious just completed what it had been told. It works precisely the same way with anything presented to it. The subconscious mind is our most valuable asset, and it is perfect. It stores all the data that we have collected over our lifetime, and it never goes away or gets misplaced.

It is our conscious mind that has trouble recalling the information that has been filed. In a relaxed state, the subconscious will provide whatever information that's requested. Pictures are the most direct way to enter information into the subconscious. For those who have mastered visualization, they will see things manifest much quicker than most. This is why what we allow into our eye gate is so important. Anything seen is being poured directly into the subconscious, and it will never be forgotten. Bad pictures, bad habits, bad input give you bad output. Garbage in, garbage out, so to speak.

This is why it is crucial to get control of your thoughts, your words and what you allow into your eye gate. Yet, these are the same tools that can be used to have everything you desire on purpose. There are three major things that shape our destiny. All things start with what we think. What we think shapes all other characteristics of who we become. Our thoughts create an emotional feeling.

Whether a positive emotional feeling or a negative one, it begins to formulate bits and pieces of your character.

That is why the Bible says in Philippians 4:8, "Whatever things are true, whatever things *are* noble, whatever things *are* just, whatever things are pure, whatever things *are* lovely, whatever things *are* of good report, if *there is* any virtue and if *there is* anything praiseworthy—meditate on these things."

Only think about the things you want in life or the person that you want to become. Whatever you think about all day long is what you will become. Since God has given us that ability to control our thoughts, we can hold any thought that we choose. So why not choose thoughts that will elevate your life?

Billy Graham wrote a book entitled *The Holy Spirit Activating God's Power in Your Life* in which he wrote a story of two wolves inside us whom we constantly battle with. The story goes like this:

> "An old Cherokee grandfather is telling his grandson a story. 'A fight is going on inside me,' he said. 'It is a terrible fight between two wolves. One is evil — he is anger, envy, greed, arrogance, resentment, lies, and ego.' He continued, 'The other is good — he is joy, peace, love, hope, serenity, humility, kindness, empathy, generosity, truth, compassion, and faith. The wolves are fighting to the death.' Wide-eyed, the boy asks his grandfather which wolf will win. The old Cherokee simply replied, 'The one you feed.'"

Now think about the real significance of this story. Each and every minute of every single day we have to decide which wolf we are going to feed. It is completely in our control. Whichever one you feed is going to determine how fruitful your life will be.

This story is very similar to what Paul says in Romans 8:9-11: "This I say then, Walk in the Spirit, and ye shall not fulfil the lust of the flesh. For the flesh lusteth against the Spirit, and the Spirit against the flesh: and these are contrary the one to the other: so that ye cannot do the things that ye would. But if ye be led of the Spirit, ye are not under the law. Now the works of the flesh are manifest, which are these; Adultery, fornication, uncleanness, lasciviousness, Idolatry, witchcraft, hatred, variance, emulations, wrath, strife, seditions, heresies, envyings, murders, drunkenness, revelings, and such like: of the which I tell you before, as I have also told you in time past, that they which do such things shall not inherit the kingdom of God. But the fruit of the Spirit is love, joy, peace, longsuffering, gentleness, goodness, faith, Meekness, temperance: against such there is no law. And they that are Christ's have crucified the flesh with the affections and lusts. If we live in the Spirit, let us also walk in the Spirit. Let us not be desirous of vain glory, provoking one another, envying one another."

This clearly gives us a great illustration of the internal conflict and the effect of choosing to live by the Spirit Man or flesh. There will always be a warring of flesh and spirit, because the flesh is earthly while the spirit is Heavenly. This is why we must come to terms with the challenge we are faced with so that we can always be mentally aware that every choice we make is vital, and those choices definitely shape who we become. When we know, we are prepared, and when we are prepared, transcending to our level of greatness is inevitable.

It will initially take some effort to achieve a level of discipline to choose rightly all the time, but like anything, the more this is exercised, the easier it becomes. Then a shift happens and a light bulb goes off in your mind, finally giving you the understanding that you and you alone can have all that you desire. You are now changed forever. If you won't be better tomorrow than you are today, then what do you need tomorrow for? (Page 168). Why exist in your purpose if you are not finding ways daily to excel in your purpose?

God provided tools in the form of laws to help us not only achieve all that he created for us to do, but continue in faithfully perfecting our skills. I really want to reiterate the significance of understanding that there is power in what you say. God gives a perfect example of this back in the book of Genesis, when he spoke the Heaven and the earth into existence.

In the beginning, God created Heaven and the earth. Verse 3 says, "And God said, 'Let there be light,' and there was light." God saw the light that it was good. Throughout the whole creation in Genesis, it started with "And God said" and ended with "And it was so." Everything that He spoke materialized.

This is why the law of confession works. God has created us in His image after His likeness. So what happens when you confess something? Well, first let's take a look at what the word "confession" means. There are many different definitions depending on the context. This is the definition relevant to this example. According to the Webster 1828 dictionary, confession means "to own avow or acknowledge, publicly to declare a belief in and adherence to, to own, to acknowledge, to declare to be true, or to admit or assent to in words." The interesting segment of this definition that I particularly want to draw your attention to is "to own, to acknowledge and to declare to be true." So when you confess something, you own what you have confessed.

When you go to a store and purchase an item, you take ownership of that item. When you go into the store to buy that item, you go to where the item is, you choose the item and then you pay for the item. You can now do whatever you please with that item. You can give away, enjoy it or throw it away. It is yours to do with as you please.

Words begin with a thought. In your mind, you have placed an inventory of thoughts. These are the items in your store. You chose these thoughts or items from whatever source: a book, a friend, your pastor, father, or mother. Regardless, you are responsible for the ones that you have housed there. You stocked every piece of inventory placed there.

Now in order to pull that thought from one of the storage bins of your mind, you must decide which one to select. You shuffle through all that inventory to find one significant for your purpose. Once it has been selected, it is then placed onto the process freeway looking for an exit. It locates that speaking device called your mouth and exits. The thought has now been spoken, and what has been spoken has been created the moment it was spoken. The materialization of what you have spoken is already on its way to you in the very near or foreseeable future. It does not have to be repeated or spoken a multitude of times. When Jesus called Lazarus out from the tomb, he said, "Lazarus, come forth," and Lazarus rose up out of that grave. It was created the moment you spoke it, and will manifest according to your level of faith.

All it takes is for you to wholeheartedly believe what you have spoken, and it has to manifest. God created our words to work exactly that way. God said, "Let the waters under the heaven be gathered together to one place, and let the dry land appear: and it was so." The word "was" is past tense, which means the instant He spoke it, it became.

Mark 11:22-23 says, "For verily I say unto you, that whoever shall say unto this mountain, be thou removed, and be thou cast into the sea; and shall not doubt in his heart, but shall believe that those things which he saith shall come to pass; he shall have whatsoever he saith."

When you understand the true power of your words coupled with faith, you will begin to choose them more wisely, because regardless of what you say, you have created something and it will show up in your life. God tells us in Hosea 4:6 that "my people are destroyed because of lack of knowledge." The verse goes on to say, "Because thou hast rejected knowledge, I shall also reject thee."

It is imperative to continue seeking knowledge and especially the mysteries of the Kingdom. You can only operate in what you know, and the only way to know is by seeking. Pastor Bill Winston wrote an entire book entitled *The Law of Confession*. This would be a great book to have in your library. Make it a practice to speak only those things that you want in life. Death and life are in the power of the tongue; therefore, speak life. Speaking things into existence is one thing, but recognizing what to do and when to do it is just as important.

The law of recognition is seeing what is necessary in your immediate environment to fulfill your life's purpose. People overlook things all the time. Most overlook talents and abilities within themselves or don't see the God-given value in others. In his book *The Law of Recognition*, Mike Murdock states, "Everything you need or want is already in your life—merely awaiting your recognition of it."

The most common mistake that we make is looking outside ourselves for what we need to succeed. God knew exactly what you were before you were born, and He put everything in you to fulfill your purpose. God placed each of us here for a reason. He provided all of the necessary tools within you for the capability of achieving what He placed you here to do.

Ever heard the old adage that anything you don't use you lose? This goes for every single area of your life. Think about it. You learned algebra, calculus and trigonometry in school. It got to the point that it came to you easily back then. You might have even been an A student in every one of these topics. Fast-forward to now. You've not used any of these math skills for the past ten years. As a matter of fact, you haven't even given it a thought. Can you honestly sit down right now at your kitchen table and solve any algebra, calculus or trigonometry problems? Having difficulty recalling the formulas that you learned so long ago? Out of sight, out of mind, so to speak. What you don't use, you lose.

Think about anything that you have not done for a while regardless of what it is. Remember when Michael Jordan, the greatest basketball player of all time, went into retirement and decided in 1994 to pursue his dreams to play major league baseball? When he returned to the Chicago Bulls in 1995, he was a totally different player and it was obvious that his basketball skills were a little rusty. He had not been on the basketball court in a couple of years. He had to work to regain what he had lost during his time off. Anything you do not use, you lose.

It's the same principle with the law of recognition. You must pay attention to the people, places and opportunities that God puts directly in your path. Every single person, place or opportunity that you come across has something to do with directing you towards your purpose. Sometimes, the key to reaching your next level life has to do with what is already around you. When you spend too much time looking beyond your own surroundings, you miss the golden nuggets that are right within your grasps.

Mike Murdock tells a story in *Law of Recognition* that took place back in the 1860s. This couple decided to sell their farmhouse and all that they had to go search for gold. They travelled all around the world. Years later, they ended up in England—bankrupt. Sometime later, they decided to go back to America to see what their old farmhouse looked like.

To their surprise, the property was surrounded by a barbed wire fence and heavily guarded with armed guards. The second largest goldmine on the North American continent, Sutter's Mill, had been discovered under their old farmhouse. Imagine what had to be to going through their minds. They sold their farmhouse to go search for gold, but it was right there under their home. A simple mineral survey of the land would have allowed them to discover what they had right under their feet. Everything we need to get to where we are going is right within our grasps. All we have to do is pay attention and recognize that it's there.

Another relevant story that he talked about in his book was one he had read in a newspaper. A man noticed a $2.39 picture frame at a flea market. He loved the frame, but hated the picture. When he got home, he took out the picture to replace it. There was another picture behind the ugly one. He thought, *this looks different. This looks like the work of a professional.* When he called the museum, he was instructed to bring it in for evaluation. They did some research, and discovered that it was the work of a famous painter. He sold it for $11 million. Something you are not seeing is costing you (page 26).

How many opportunities have been right under your nose that have been overlooked or simply ignored because you were looking beyond rather than what was already in front of you? Having a vision of where you are going is a very good thing; however, mastering where you are as you are working towards your vision allows you to see what you already have to assist you on your journey. Every end goal has a series of steps or stages before its actual achievement.

Michael Jordan did not become a six-time NBA champion his first year in the NBA. He had to take a series of steps to learn how to become a champion. Jordan lost in the playoffs six seasons in a row before overcoming the Bad Boys Detroit Pistons in 1991. His end goal was to win a championship, and the process of losing gave him an education about what it took to get to that level. Once Michael Jordan figured out the system of winning, he ended up with six championships.

He had a team of people around him that helped him fulfill that vision. It is no different with you. It takes others to help you along the way. Whether it is reading books, having mentors, close friendships, your parents or blood relatives, many of those in your circle are key to your success. Not everyone in your circle is there to provide positive support for the achievement of your vision. Some are there to disrupt, attack and destroy; however, they too can be useful.

Adversity strengthens and molds certain aspects of who you are, making you more resilient and determined to successfully create what you have spoken. Joseph shared his vision to those closest to him, and in spite of the envy, jealousy and manipulation, they could not stop him from accomplishing the vision that God had placed in him.

Joseph recognized opportunities even in the direst situations. The Bible tells of a story about a wealthy Egyptian man's wife's attempt to seduce Joseph. He was placed in an awkward situation because the rich man had entrusted Joseph to oversee his entire estate to include his household. As she made her advances towards Joseph, he refused and immediately ran out of the room. The queen was embarrassed, infuriated and vengeful. She told the rich man that Joseph tried to rape her, and Joseph was thrown in prison.

This would have sorely affected most, but because Joseph operated with integrity, he was quickly given oversight of all the prisoners by the keeper of the prison. There were two men thrown into prison by the king. One was a chief butler and the other a chief baker. They had been in prison now for a little while. Each man had a dream on the same night. Both became sad because there was no one to interpret their dreams.

Joseph noticed that they were both in a somber mood and asked them why they seemed so sad. They shared with Joseph their dreams. He recognized a golden opportunity and quickly responded with a question: "Do not interpretations belong to God?" He shared with the chief butler the meaning of his dream. In three days, he was to be restored to his position in the king's palace. In return, he asked that he remember him when he was reunited with the king. The chief butler agreed that he would honor Joseph's request.

When the chief baker realized that the first interpretation was accurate, he also shared his dream with Joseph. Unfortunately, the chief baker was looking at a very different outcome. It was interpreted that, in three days, the chief baker was to be beheaded and his body hung on a tree to be eaten by birds.

The chief butler was restored to his original position just as Joseph had interpreted; yet, the chief butler did not keep his word and he forgot about Joseph. He remained in prison two more years after the chief butler's release.

Then one night, the king had a disturbing dream and was in desperate search for an interpreter, but there were none. The chief butler recalled what Joseph had done for him while in prison and told the king. After hearing from the chief butler that Joseph had accurately interpreted his own and the chief baker's dreams, the king summoned for Joseph. As Joseph stood before the king, he was asked by the king about his ability to interpret dreams. In response, Joseph quickly let the king know that only God can interpret dreams.

Again, Joseph recognized an opportunity to change his situation. He shared with the king the interpretation of his dream and what God was about to do in the land of Egypt. Because of the interpretation, the king rewarded Joseph for the things that God had showed him. He regarded Joseph as the most wise and discreet man in all the kingdom and put Joseph over his house and all the land of Egypt. Joseph endured in spite of overwhelming challenges of being thrown in a hole to die by his own family, sold into slavery, accused of attempted rape, thrown into prison and lied to by the chief butler.

He remained humble in spirit and open to opportunities afforded him. He never pushed his way into his destiny. His destiny came calling regardless of his situation. He kept a positive attitude and his eyes open so that he could recognize opportunities as they were presented.

Everything you need, you already have. You have enough intelligence, you have enough confidence, you have the right connections and you already know enough people and have the eternal guidance of the Holy Spirit. You don't need anything more. You don't need further education. You don't need more money. And you don't need for someone to give you a break.

All you need to do is decide, do and finish whatever it is that you have set out to do. Recognize what you already have, and start right where you are. Everything else you need will come at the right time in the right place from the right people.

Live your life with purpose. Conquer your projects with enthusiasm, and walk out your life as if you have something of value to do. Don't be easily discouraged. Catastrophes will come. Harsh winds will sometimes blow and raging storms will appear, but none of these is enough to rob you of your purpose. Your purpose can't be derailed by circumstances, unfavorable conditions or unforeseen events. The only thing that can affect your living out your purpose is the person looking back at you in the mirror.

Regardless of what endeavor we take on in life, we must learn the value of operating in the law of excellence. Having the attitude of doing all things in excellence will honor those whom you serve and expedite your journey towards your destiny. A perfect example of this in the Bible is the story of Daniel.

Daniel had an excellent spirit, and he chose to do all things in excellence even when no one was watching. King Nebuchadnezzar of Babylon instructed his master of eunuchs to bring children out of Israel who were of the king's seed and princes.

"Excellent Spirit of Daniel

Children in whom was no blemish, but well favoured, and skillful in all wisdom, and cunning in knowledge, and understanding science, and such as had ability in them to stand in the king's palace, and whom they might teach the learning and the tongue of the Chaldeans."

—Daniel 1:4 KJV

"There is a man in your kingdom in whom is the spirit of the holy gods. In the days of your father, light and understanding and wisdom like the wisdom of the gods were found in him, and King Nebuchadnezzar, your father—your father the king—made him chief of the magicians, enchanters, Chaldeans, and astrologers, [12] because an excellent spirit, knowledge, and understanding to interpret dreams, explain riddles, and solve problems were found in this Daniel, whom the king named Belteshazzar. Now let Daniel be called, and he will show the interpretation."

—Daniel 5:11-12 KJV

"It pleased Darius to set over the kingdom an hundred and twenty princes, which should be over the whole kingdom; And over these three presidents; of whom Daniel was first: that the princes might give accounts unto them, and the king should have no damage. Then this Daniel was preferred above the presidents and princes, because an excellent spirit was in him; and the king thought to set him over the whole realm. Then the presidents and princes sought to find occasion against Daniel concerning the kingdom; but they could find none occasion nor fault; forasmuch as he was faithful, neither was there any error or fault found in him."

—Daniel 6:1-4 KJV

Daniel gained favor of God because he lived a life of excellence. God elevated Daniel above all in the provinces except the king. Darius the King trusted Daniel to oversee the entire kingdom without any doubt or worry, all because of his lifelong example of walking in excellence.

Operating in the spirit of excellence serves all who encounter it. God is honored, those whom you serve are given honor and you are highly respected and honored. We make a decision to function in excellence in every area of our lives not because of what it does for us but because of whom it honors when we do.

We serve a mighty God and everything we do is in honor of Him, and when we honor God, we honor everything else we associate with. All those who we come into contact will know whom we serve by our actions.

When we walk in a spirit of excellence, the favor of God drapes over us without fail. Which brings me to my last point. As born-again Christians, we have the law of favor on our lives.

The law of favor is the grace of God. It is God giving us the ability to do what we ordinarily could not do. For instance, salvation is of the Lord, and since it is a free gift of God, we can only receive it of Him.

"For by grace are ye saved through faith; and that not of yourselves: it is the gift of God: Not of works, lest any man should boast."

—Ephesians 2:8 KJV

It is also the favor of God that He provided an avenue for us to regain our relationship even after the fall of man through sin. He still sent Jesus down here on earth to die an anguishing, humiliating death for the sin of the world—not just the born-again believers, but the whole world.

God's favor is not anything that we deserve. It is God's love and grace that still affords us this benevolent act of kindness.

God granting man eternal life is a prime example of His favor on our lives—unmerited favor. God did not have to set things up for man to ever see Heaven or have eternal life, but he did.

God wants to give you the desires of your heart, but you—his creation—must believe that we can have anything we want . . . on purpose.

CHAPTER TEN

There are Diamonds in the Midst

D on't look for diamonds in a faraway country when they are right under your feet. There was a story of a farmer who had a lovely stream that flowed right through the middle of his property. Every so often he and his wife would go down to the stream and just watch it flow. The sun would hit the water just right, and they could see little sparkles emanating throughout the stream.

One day the farmer decided to sell the farm and pursue a life of riches. Years later, he ended up in some faraway country broke and destitute. When he and his wife returned to their country, he had an inkling to go by the old farm to see how things were going. When he arrived there, the property was no longer accessible because it was now heavily guarded. He discovered that the old farm was now the second largest diamond mine in North America. The sparkles that used to reflect off of the sunlight from that stream were diamonds. Beneath that stream was a huge diamond mine. The farmer was in disbelief.

Many times, the very thing that we are looking for is right under our noses. That idea that you never wrote, the human connections you could have made, that $3 picture you bought at the yard sale, the land you own or that old car your grand-dad gave to you are all right at your fingertips; yet you fail to recognize their value. Why? It could be a lack of expertise about the items you possess. It could be your failure to pay attention to detail. You may not like asking someone else to evaluate your stuff, and, for whatever reason, you never come to realize that you already have value at your disposal.

You may own something of value that has not yet been properly assessed. You may already have the relationships you need to help you move to that next level. You may have a multi-million-dollar idea sitting in that cavity right behind your forehead, called your subconscious mind.

You've most likely been prompted many times in your life to go to this place or that place or to go say hello to that person at the party or launch a new idea, but somehow you managed to always talk yourself out of it. You weren't really sure why, but you just know that you did. Oftentimes, it was because it was easier. You didn't have to veer off into unknown territory. You stayed in your most comfortable place: the familiar. If you are going do anything of great significance, you must find a way to overcome being comfortable.

Discovering those things around you takes keen observation and a willingness to ask yourself tough questions. What are my weaknesses? What are some of the things that I do well? What do I have in my possession right now to get started doing what I desire to do? Do I have access to some or all of what I need? What are my biggest fears, and why? What price am I willing to pay to get the things that I want in life? What sacrifices are acceptable to complete this journey? What are my priorities and in what order?

These are crucial questions that should be answered before pursuing your dreams. If you take that valuable time to ask and find answers to the right questions before you start, it will give you the resilience to overcome unexpected events, the fortitude to work through life as its happening and remain driven. The reality that no journey, no matter how easy or how hard, can be successful without first giving yourself an honest, in-depth assessment and without counting the cost.

Luke 14:28-30 says, "For which of you, intending to build a tower, sitteth not down first, and counteth the cost, whether he have sufficient to finish it? Lest haply, after he hath laid the foundation, and is not able to finish it, all that behold it begin to mock him, Saying, This man began to build, and was not able to finish." Counting the cost before any journey regardless of what it is will better set you up for success.

As you are walking through your journey, many will be watching. Some will be watching in excitement with much support, while some will be observing waiting for you to fail. They will all be friendly and appear to be supportive, but even those who are secretly hoping that you fail can't affect where you are going as long as your plans and your steps to get there remain with you and only you. No one else needs to know the details of how you are going to do what it is that you have decided. The less information they have, the less likely it will be that they can sabotage your plans. Tell only those that you trust and that truly support what you are doing; otherwise, no one else needs to know the path you have chosen to arrive at your destination.

As you are working towards achieving your dream, create realistic goals and timelines for its attainment. You must understand how you finish in order to reach your final destination. Look back over your life and think about all the things that you have completed. What were they? How difficult were they? What were you motivated by? How did you feel when you finished? Use every positive memory that you have of your completing something. Then take the time to evaluate the hows and whys of each success. It is just as valuable to assess any major failures in your life. When you understand why you failed, you can avert repeating that same scenario going forward.

Why does this matter? You need to look deep inside yourself so that you can know beyond a shadow of a doubt what is in you that makes you see something all the way through. Some have an overall vision that they see in their mind's eye continuously. Some write out their vision with pen and paper, and read over it several times a day. Many create vision boards with pictures of each goal that they must complete. Whatever method you use, make sure that it is in alignment with your personality type. This is very important. You must figure out what drives you to do the things that you do not want to do but must do.

Something must be in your life that will motivate you to move beyond those things that are not fun for you to do. Not everything you do while journeying towards your goal will be joyful. There will be setbacks. There will be days where things don't go quite as planned. Some days you will have to do things that you absolutely hate doing. Suck it up and do it regardless of how you feel about it, because this part is also necessary in helping to accomplish what you have set out to do.

Remember this is not someone else's vision, and handing the dirty work over to someone else doesn't mean that they will do the job that's needed for you to move forward. They may hate doing the chore you assigned them as much as you do. The difference is, you have a vision and they are not living in your vision. They don't have to work through it. They don't see what you are seeing, so there is absolutely zero motivation for them to even have a concern about completing the task. Learn to work past those things that you hate to do so that you can create a life of only doing those things that you love to do.

I recall back in the late seventies, I was a young soldier stationed at Fort Knox, Kentucky. I was an exceptional soldier, and my master sergeant chose me to go through primary leadership training. It was a very difficult training academy. It was a school for enlisted soldiers to eventually start transitioning into officers' school.

One of the things we had to complete before graduating was a field trip through very rough terrain, mostly wooded areas. At some point, to shave time off of the course, we had to run pretty much full speed through trees, brush, through ravines and inclines. I absolutely hated running through the woods.

There were skunks, snakes and various other wild animals that you had to contend with while maintaining your bearings running at almost full speed. The only thing that kept me focused on doing this thing that I hated with a passion was my desire to complete this course because of a promise I had made to my master sergeant. My word meant something to me, and that alone drove me to get past that one thing that I dreaded. Because I stood for what I had promised, I excelled far beyond my own expectations.

At the end of the course, the leadership got together and voted on who was the top cadet during the eight weeks of training. They could only choose one soldier for distinguished grad and one for honor grad. There were about 150 cadets chosen nationwide for this training. There were rangers, presidential guards, green berets and others participating in this leadership course. Out of all these exceptional cadets, I was chosen for both the distinguished and the honor grad during that eight-week training session.

I was totally shocked, and yet very excited. I had no clue that I had performed at a level high enough to surpass every other cadet there. My main objective was to complete a course I had promised to complete, but another part of me also thought that, if I was going to be there, I might as well do each and every part to the very best of my ability. Either way, I was going to have to exert the energy, so I might as well give it my all.

It paid off in a huge way. From that point on, I have adapted that attitude in everything I do. To this day, when I am struggling doing things that I don't like to do, I think about my running full speed through those woods, hating every step and dreading running into some animal and spooking them into a frenzy to bite me, attack me or spray me. I did that thing that I hated and came out on the other side as an honor student and a distinguished grad.

What price are you willing to pay to achieve your vision? Everyone has it in them to motivate themselves whenever struggles come. It does take considerable effort to search out what drives you past those dreadful tasks into a place of knowing that, no matter what, you will complete what you have started.

Your real strength of character will be exposed the instant that you recognize that your mind is by far the most effective and most critical asset that you have. Once your mind is truly set on the achievement of a goal or vision, it will create avenues that place you on a path for success. It does not matter what your endeavor is. If you can reasonably do what it is that you are seeking to do, your mind will find ways according to your talents and abilities to reshape you.

It won't be necessary for you to seek outside of yourself for the things you need. You will be directed time and time again to every person, place or thing that you need to fulfill that burning desire towards your vision. Your senses will be magnified, and as you maneuver your way through a maze of past assumptions and self-doubt, you will find resources, professional advice, doors opened, blessings dropped and opportunities unfold.

Your subconscious mind is now engaged with your conscious mind, carving away all those past failures and crippling mindsets. You are now transitioning into the person you've envisioned as you move closer and closer to your final destination. Your subconscious is an overflowing diamond mine waiting for you to summon its extraordinary powers to help you manifest all that you desire.

Diamonds are in your midst. At some point, you have to trust what God designed you to be. There will be many folks out there who will be happy to tell you what you can't do. Don't allow yourself to be discouraged. Go out and do it anyway. There will be times when you may feel overwhelmed, and that's okay. Any time you take on something life-changing of any significance, there are stages during the process where you are going to feel the enormity of it all. Push on. Revamp your plan and keep pushing on.

You will get plenty of relief when it is all over and done with. Challenge yourself to operate outside your comfort zone. Do things that you normally wouldn't do. The more you do this, the better prepared you will be in handling unexpected catastrophes. They will come. Others around you will be watching and judging. Some will be silently hoping that you fail. It's all okay. When others criticize you, they are simply disguising their own fears. The only thing that matters is how you feel about what you are doing and whether you really have faith in your ability to finish what you have started.

John Maxwell said it best in his book *The 15 Invaluable Laws of Growth* (page 96). Someone else's opinion of you does not have to become your reality. Remember back in high school when the most important thing was being accepted or feeling like you were a part of something? The popular kids made fun of and harassed those considered weird or different.

Now fast-forward twenty years, and what you will most likely find is that those popular kids back in high school very seldom fair well as adults; however, those who were labeled weirdos or geeks are usually doing far better in every facet of life. I did not realize this myself until I became an adult, but even back then, all of the harassment, ridicule and intimidations stemmed from fear. Most nerds were straight A students who pretty much kept to themselves and stayed out of trouble. They weren't comfortable being in the limelight, so to speak. They had better things to do like studying or making plans about what they wanted to do after their high school years.

Don't ever take others' snide remarks or making fun of you at face value, because most often, what you'll find is a hidden fear of who you are or what you are about to become. Human nature is a beast, but like any beast out in the wild, you can avoid it or end up being devoured by it.

Be too busy doing what you need to do for accomplishing your goals to worry about someone else's insecurities or fears. Don't be impolite or lower yourself to their level, but be cognizant of what they are doing and why. More likely than not, you will find that the issue is really never about you and your journey, but them and their internal battles about their own capabilities.

Comparing yourself to others is *not* the magic formula for success. We have all lived different lives and taken different paths. Even if people have had very similar lives and crossed almost identical paths, their DNA is still coded differently.

They were raised up with different parents, different role models, different philosophies and different perspectives. Regardless of how similar they may seem on the outside, they were built much differently on the inside. Everything we do or don't do has to do with what was molded and shaped on the inside of us.

One may have been raised to clearly understand the value of choices and their ability to make them, while another may have had the upbringing of feeling like choices for them were limited and that they were not in control. And that alone is the key component, isn't it? Coming to a place in life where you know that choice is totally in your control regardless of your upbringing or environment. But how do you get there if you were reared in an impoverished, deprived state most of your life? Everywhere you turn, there are negative images splashed across television screens. Newspapers print derogatory stories depicting only violence and incarceration for people who look like you. You've never been exposed to anything but destitution and depravity. You've not seen positive images of yourself nor had role models in your life that you could learn from.

The first thing that you need to recognize is that you are created in the image of God just like every other human being on planet earth. The exact same DNA that God breathed into Adam exists also in you. The same rights that God granted Adam were also passed on to you. Secondly, whatever it is that you want to do in life has already been done by someone who looks just like you. Research those who have come before you who have done what you want to do. See what they did that was successful, and do exactly that. Do not reinvent the wheel. If it worked for them, it will work for you.

One of the most well-known writers of our time started their journey in Joplin, Missouri, in the early 1900s. His parents divorced when they were but a young child, and his father moved to Mexico. He was raised by his grandparents until age thirteen, and then moved to Lincoln, Illinois, to live with their mother and her husband until eventually settling down in Cleveland, Ohio. After graduating high school, he lived a short stint in Mexico before landing in New York City to attend the University of Columbia. While there, he held various odd jobs as a busboy, an assistant cook and a laundryman. Eventually, taking on a position as a seaman, he travelled to Africa and throughout Europe.

In 1924, he ended up in Washington, DC, where he wrote his first book entitled *The Weary Blues*, which was published in 1926 by Alfred A. Knopf. Three years later, he completed his college education at Lincoln University in Pennsylvania. Shortly after, in 1930, he finished his first novel *Not without Laughter*, which won the Harmon Gold Medal for literature. He asserted that he was influenced by

Paul Lawrence Dunbar, Carl Sandburg and Walt Whitman. We all know this person by the name of Langston Hughes. His writing gave us a clear depiction of the African American plight from the 1920s through the 1960s. The way he lived and his life's work had a huge impact in forging the artistic contributions of the Harlem Renaissance of the 1920's. His talent left an imprint on our culture and will forever be cherished. If you don't have mentors around you, or you don't have access to any, there is a whole lot of written material out there on anything and everything. They can now become your mentors. Another option is to decide to be a pioneer. There is nothing wrong with being the first to start something, be something or do something. Everything that's ever been accomplished had to be started by somebody. In March of 1827, two guys by the names of John Russwurm and Samuel Cornish launched the first African American owned and operated newspaper. We were still subjected to Jim Crow laws in the 1950's, so can you imagine the hardships they faced in 1827? They paved the way for many other black-owned establishments to include the *Chicago Defender* (1870), *Essence Magazine, Jet Magazine, Black Enterprise* and the *Source.* Jackie Robinson was the first black baseball player in the modern era. Robert L. Johnson, the owner of Black Entertainment Television, became the first black billionaire. Senator Barack Obama battled against all odds to become the first black president of these United States. If it hasn't yet been done, then go ahead and be the first. Whatever it is that you decide to do, don't let the past stop you. Just because there are rules in place today, it doesn't mean that they won't change tomorrow. It doesn't matter what the obstacles are when working towards your goals. You can take them head on. Find the appropriate resources to assist you, or circumvent them altogether. There is an old saying: "Where there is a will, there is a way." If your desire is strong enough to achieve that which you have decided, no mountains, valleys or stone walls will stop you. Don't ever give another person the right to hinder your dreams. Always ask yourself, "What can I do to achieve the things that I want? How can I do this, or how can I do that?" Change your language from "I can't do, be or have" to "How can I do, be or have?" If you ask different questions, I guarantee that you will get different results.

Your subconscious already has all the answers that you are seeking. This part of our mind has access far beyond our limited space. All you have to do to utilize this magnificent tool given to us by God Himself is ask the right questions and it will find you an answer.

Many of us have read the scripture in the Bible about the spirit knowing all things. Yet, I am not sure that many of us actually believe that is true. The only way to be sure is to test it, right? Ask yourself any question at bedtime right before sleep, and you will be amazed at what happens. This part of your mind works diligently while you are sleeping.

It controls all of your bodily functions as you rest. Your heart still beats, you still breathe air, your food that you ate earlier that evening is still digesting, your skin still sweats and your sense of smell, taste, touch and hearing are all still functioning. Nothing rests in sleep. Your subconscious mind is handling it all so that you can rest in peace. But it is also doing something else. Your mind is still working on the problems of the day and the issues that are yet unresolved.

It is searching, calculating and solving as you are asleep. It never stops working, and it never rests until it solves what it has been given. "Ask and it shall be given you, seek and you shall find, knock and the door shall be opened unto you. For everyone that asketh, receiveth and to him who seeks, he shall find and to him who knocketh, the door shall be opened." This is scriptural. This is the Word of God.

The subconscious mind is our worker bee. Albert Einstein, who was one of the most brilliant mathematicians of our time, solved many problems while sleeping. The mind, like the ocean, has never been thoroughly explored. It does so much more than we can ever imagine. It is a recorded fact that we use very little of our brain and 95 percent of it lives in the subconscious mind.

Scientists have no clue what the capabilities are of the subconscious mind because it can't be evaluated by any known method. The myth is that we only use 10 percent of our brain power. It has been documented that scientists only understand about 10 percent of what our brain actually does. What about the other 90 percent? It is constantly working, processing millions of bits of data per second, making decisions and finding answers to thousands of queries simultaneously.

It is busy creating those magnificent pictures of how you want your life to be. It is tirelessly and relentlessly searching, seeking and creating while, at the same time, controlling all of your key bodily functions like your breathing, your heartbeat, your balance as you walk. It's judging distances, deciphering information of every sort and on alert for unexpected actions or events.

Although the subconscious mind does an enormous amount of work, it still needs some direction from you as to the things that you want in life. It must have a clear, concise picture of what you want your future self to look like. For many, failing to connect what you think and inaction will not produce what it is that you want. Thought and action must complement each other if you ever expect the manifestation of the life you have imagined.

By consistently thinking on those things that you want, they eventually will be drawn towards you. Bits and pieces of information will trickle in as needed, and you will begin to actualize your goals. New relationships will develop, and people that you don't even know will be compelled to offer knowledge and resources that support your journey.

Your new connections will do their part by providing you exactly what you need when you need it. Thinking alone will not make the things that you wish for a reality without the work of your hands. The two must coincide with one another, and your thoughts along with actions must work in perfect harmony. One without the other will have you spinning in circles and ending up in the same place with the same old results, never moving towards what it is that you want.

Test the current reality that you are living in. If it does not align with your vision, you are not synchronizing your thoughts and your actions, and you are in disharmony. I can't emphasize enough how important it is for these to work in concert with one another. One of the most indelible facts is that we very seldom get what we want. You get what you expect.

If the internal conversation does not match the words being spoken, the materialization of your desires will not manifest. When you hear someone saying all the right things and see the opposite of what they have showing up in their lives, it becomes obvious that what they believe and what they are saying are not in alignment. Faith in what you are saying will manifest in your life without fail.

CHAPTER ELEVEN

Speak Your New Life Now

Have faith that every word you have spoken has already gone forth to do what you have confessed. When we wake up in the morning, we have started a new day. Our past is behind us, and God willing, our future is ahead of us. We can't relive our past, and we do not yet have a future.

The only time we have is the present. So everything we speak should be spoken in the context of having it now: seeing it, touching it and experiencing it right now. We can imagine our future all we want, but there are no guarantees that we will ever see that future.

We can dwell on the past reliving all those good times that we had. We can rekindle those loving memories or those exciting fun-filled vacations. We can choose to concentrate on all those painstaking bumps in the road, past failures and missed opportunities. But why exert valuable energy and focus on a past you can't change or imagine a future that may not ever come?

Instead, use every second of your precious time and energy living the life that you want to live right here—in your present moment. As you are living the life you have envisioned as if it has already materialized, your present moment will become the life you have imagined.

Initially, this may be a very difficult concept to understand, but this is exactly what God is telling us when He says, "Call those things that be not as though they were." Living the life that you have imagined as if it is already here starts doing some things to you psychologically. It tells your subconscious mind that you already have what you have imagined. Once that deep-rooted belief is intertwined with what you have imagined, your subconscious will automatically bring things into alignment materially. This is by far the most valued component of having everything that you say with immovable faith.

Living life in the present as if you already have what you have envisioned may appear very strange to those on the outside looking in. They have absolutely no clue what you are working with and how you are going to end up.

The revelation that has been given you does not yet exist in them and may never be something comprehensible from their point of view. None of that is important to you, nor should their viewpoint hinder the life you are living. Others will always try to figure out why you do what you do. They will assess everything about you.

Those who support you will try to better understand what you are doing and where you are going because they want to do their part in helping you along your journey. Others will be looking for ways to poke holes in your dream. They will attempt to tear down your confidence in who you are, or deliberately sabotage what they can when they can. They will try to figure out how you are doing what you are doing with what you have got when they have no clue what you have got. But somewhere along the line, you will have to live your life regardless of your private enemies or a zero-support system.

When those around you don't understand what you are working with, rather than ask you, they will just fill in the blanks with their own interpretations. They are most always 100 percent wrong in their perception. This has no bearing on your living your life in the present moment as if you already have the life that you have imagined.

When you live the life that you imagined in the present, you have pulled your future to the present. This whole deception about getting to a future does not create that future. It is living and feeling your future in the present that manifests the life you have imagined, and that is the key.

Many of us have been systematically indoctrinated to envision a future that we are always chasing without ever bringing it to actualization. We've been blatantly misguided on how to bring those things that we have imagined into our present. Constantly imagining a life that you are hoping to get to will never give you that life; living your life now as if you already have those things that you are imagining will.

The reason that we fail to see the life we have imagined in our present moment is that we are reaching for something far away rather than creating what's available to us now. Most of what you believe you see in the future and are chasing already exists right where you are. If it is not available to you within the grasp of your own resources, then it is accessible to you from the connections in your circle.

In order to recognize what you already have to live your future life now, you must first be familiar with every person, place or thing that you have access to. Living your future life now requires a keen awareness of what God has already given you. Very seldom do we truly take stock in what we already possess. We should always start right in the very spot that we are standing. This is where your present moment is.

"There is always something that you can do right now to move closer to your success. Use need, desire, ambition and attitude to motivate yourself to immediate action. Overcome thoughts of helplessness, limitation, lack, negativity, and failure."

—Herbert Harris

What we are seeing in our future is already being played out in our minds. Since what we have conceived has been believed, then it has already been achieved. Our mind is really the storehouse of our present reality. Whatever you are living in your mind you are already experiencing now. It makes no difference to your subconscious what you are envisioning and what you are actually experiencing.

It believes that you are what you are imagining; therefore, it only delivers what it believes to be true. The only true measure of time is the here and now. Anything that hasn't happened yet can't be measured in time, because it is the future that we haven't lived.

Everything that has happened is no longer relevant for the moment that we are living in. The future can't provide happiness for us now, just like the past can't change what we are experiencing in the present. Imagine using all that energy, excitement, enthusiasm and focus on the life that you are living right now. That is where all of your joy lies. This moment right now is your life—not tomorrow or yesterday but right now!

So expect the best that life has to offer now. Believe that you are who you want to be now. Be happy in what you are experiencing in this moment. It may be the only piece of life that you have left because anything can change in the blink of an eye.

> "Believe that you already have everything you need to get everything you want. You should become independent as a part of your interdependence."
>
> —Herbert Harris

On January 31, 2000, Flight 261 flying out of Puerto Vallarta, Jalisco, in Mexico to Tacoma International Airport in Seattle, Washington, was headed out on a routine flight. All the passengers that day were excited to reach their destinations. Many of them were most likely thinking about getting back home to their loved ones.

Some were flying on business and probably going over client material on the flight. Others just wanted to get to where they were going because they dreaded travelling through the air. Whatever future they were thinking about while sitting on that plane that day never happened.

All the joy of getting to where they were going was consumed in a place far from where they were. All the nervousness, anxiety, all the hope and excitement of getting to wherever Flight 261 was taking them—even with all these different thoughts floating around meandering throughout the aircraft, the pilots, airlines crew and the plane were all doing what they were designed or trained to.

The aviators of Flight 261 had 17,750 flight hours between them and over 4,000 flight hours with the MD-83 model. Prior to this day, Flight 261 had logged 26,584 flight hours and 14.315 cycles with no record of mechanical issues. The plane was cruising at 31,000 feet when there was a noise heard by both the captain and the first officer that sounded like a thump. The horizontal stabilizer had jammed, and once the flight crew unjammed it to free it back up, the aircraft moved into a nose-down position and began rapidly descending in a nose-dive to around 24,000 feet in 80 seconds.

The flight crew regained control of the aircraft and began discussing plans with air traffic control about descending to about 10,000 feet to change flight configurations so that they could land at LAX airport instead of San Francisco as scheduled. The aircraft was lowered as requested, and the captain began reconfiguration to land at LAX.

After about 10 minutes, there were four distinct thumps. Seventeen seconds later, there was an extremely loud noise due to an overstrained jack screw assembly failure that separated from the acme nut holding it in place. The aircraft descended 18,000 feet in an inverted nose-dive in 81 seconds. A few seconds later, it crashed in the Pacific Ocean killing all 88 people on board.

Every single person on Flight 261 that day most likely had plans of a future. Many of them probably lived for that future most of their waking hours, and yet, the moment that overstrained jack-screw assembly gave way and separated from the acme nut, the future that most of them imagined would never materialize for them or their loved ones.

We all have heard it said that we could die at any time and that the next day is not promised, yet, for some reason, we live life as though we have all the time in the world. Living in the future does not prevent the day of our appointed time. We can choose to keep reaching for a future not yet lived, or we can pull that future into the present.

The future is too far away to enjoy, but you can absolutely have a great time in the present. You can choose to live exactly how you want to live right now. Remove barriers or limitations that are preventing you from living a full life right now, in this moment.

Go back to that vivid imagination that you had when you were a child. Remember in an earlier chapter I mentioned that whatever you think about all day long is what you become and that what you confess and believe has happened already. When you speak what you believe in faith, and if what you say it has already happened, why not live in the moment as if it's true?

Experience the reality of the life you're living now with all your senses. If your new reality is driving an immaculate luxury car, then go test drive that luxury car. Sit in it. Feel the soft leather. Admire the quality of the wood grain panel and the gold trim. Turn on the CD player and pop in your favorite playlist just to listen to the clarity of the sound system. Smell the new leather permeating throughout the car. Touch and feel all that you can. Be bold and ask to take it for a test drive.

Of course, the salesperson is going to do everything possible to get you to walk out of there with an enormous car payment, but don't fall for it. Remember why you are there. Your sole purpose for being there is to experience everything involved with the reality of sitting behind the wheel driving the car of your dreams. Go look at the houses that you see yourself living in. Take a trip to the Ethan Allen store and pick out the furniture for your new home. Do all the things you would do as if you are already in the position to do it.

At the moment, this is your reality. It is not ten years from now or twenty years from now. It is right now. When you live your future now, something triggers your subconscious mind to respond to what you are currently living and experiencing. When it is convinced that this is your life, you'll notice that opportunities start opening up. Influential people start popping up in your life. Doors open and connections are made that you weren't seeking after but because you are living your future now, your future is materializing right before your eyes inch by inch, moment by moment, day by day.

You begin to notice that everything seems to be going your way. Things are happening that you are not striving for. You are not reaching for a future that you will never have. Because you are living your future now, it is developing now right before your eyes. There is no tremendous effort involved. There is no strife to reach a certain goal in a certain timeline. There are no bosses to please, no enemies around to sabotage your dreams. You are living all that you imagined in the very moment that you're in, and it's developing around you as you continue to live your future now.

Jim Carrey is a well-known actor/comedian today. He did something that most people would find peculiar. Jim Carrey woke up everyday living in his imagination. He always imagined himself a huge success and saw himself entertaining the world.

At the time, none of what he was imagining had shown up in his life. It did not matter. He imagined it anyway. He saw himself on a movie screen drawing large crowds at the theaters. One day in 1985, he sat down and decided to write himself a $10 million check for acting services rendered. He dated that check to be paid by November of 1995. He put that check in his wallet and forgot about it.

However, his subconscious mind did not. Just before Thanksgiving of 1995, he was offered a check for $10 million for the movie *Dumb and Dumber*. How did he make this happen? He got what he expected, and he lived out what he was believing to be true in his mind each and every day. He pulled his future into the present with his imagination.

He saw himself on the big screen day in and day out tricking his subconscious mind into that reality. He had a definite date locked in for the subconscious mind to work with. There was no confusion and no mixed messages. The check had been written and tucked away in his wallet. By doing that, he committed to his subconscious mind the amount and the timeline along with the services rendered for the attainment of those $10 million.

What Jim Carrey did was absolutely masterful, and yet, even though this method worked, many will still dismiss it because of misunderstanding of the tools that's available for all to use. Was it easy to remain focused on a future that was not yet his reality? Most likely it was very challenging, especially when you drop out of your imagination and see your material reality. He never gave up hope nor his dream of one day being a famous Hollywood actor filling the theaters worldwide.

"When you get to the end of your rope,

Tie a knot and hang on,

Be prepared to do whatever it takes,

For as long as it takes"

It is easy to shut something out that you don't understand. Why? It is not necessary to think about how it worked or why it worked or if it is even possible that it would work for you. Dismissing it keeps you in your safety zone and doesn't allow you to grow beyond your staunch disposition. It won't persuade you to veer outside your limited views in an attempt to better your life or your chances at success. That is all okay. As long as you are striving towards your future, it will always be just out of your reach.

Striving means that you are vigorously and ardently working towards something. When you're diligently pursuing something, you're living in hopes of attaining the future that you see rather than just choosing to live in that future now. Why should we even concern ourselves with living what we have imagined right now? Because tomorrow is not promised, and the future that you're chasing may never come to fruition.

On September 11, 2001, at 8:45 a.m., a lot of people's tomorrows got stripped right out from under them. Many went into the office that day as usual. There were no concerns or thoughts of not ever seeing their loved ones again. There may have been a litany of other thoughts maneuvering through their minds, but I assure you, not seeing tomorrow wasn't one of them.

I am sure that most expected to end their work day in normal fashion: get in their cars at the end of the day or catch the subway heading to their destinations. But on this day, a Boeing 767 crashed into one of the towers of the World Trade Center. They did not even have to leave the office to be a part of this unexpected terrorist attack. This aircraft was loaded with 20,000 gallons of fuel and did far more damage than expected. To their surprise, eighteen minutes later, another Boeing 767 crashed into the other twin tower. As each aircraft struck their targets, explosions erupted and fire spread quickly throughout each floor the planes plunged into. Just fifteen minutes later, both towers plummeted to the ground, leaving massive mountains of rubble and debris.

Visibility was non-existent for blocks surrounding this catastrophe. On this day, a total of 2,977 human lives were abruptly cut short. Thousands upon thousands of people were impacted by the deaths from this tragic event. All those that died that day left behind loved ones who will experience the effect for years to come.

We wake up believing that we will see another day and that life will continue on as we have planned. We create our visions and we set our goals, and we do our due diligence for their attainment only to eventually come to the realization that life can be very fragile and unpredictable. We all have done it, dangled that amazing future out in front of us continuously reaching for new heights, telling ourselves that it is all for the cause of growth.

At the end of the day, all we have is the present moment, and in essence, we can be, do or have whatever we have imagined in our future right now. With all the books I've read and all the seminars I've attended, I have finally developed the understanding that living your life gloriously doesn't have to be twenty years down the road. It doesn't have to be something that you hope to do later or dream about day in and day out until it becomes a reality.

Everything you desire can become a reality today in the moment that you are living in right now. That is pivotal. Joel Osteen wrote a book entitled *Your Best Life Now*. He gave several examples of those who are always talking about what they will do someday:

"Someday, things will be better in my life." "Someday, I'll earn more money and I won't have to worry about how I am going to pay my bills." "Someday, I'm going to get in better physical condition." "Someday, I'll have a better relationship with God and enjoy more of his goodness."

He goes on to say, "Unfortunately, 'someday' never comes." Today is the only day we have. We can't do anything about the past, and we don't know what the future holds. But we can live at our fullest potential right now! Everything that we have done in life is behind us and everything we will do in life hasn't happened yet, so regardless of what plans we have made or what goals we have set for ourselves, the only window of time relevant to our lives is right now.

> "Therefore take no thought for tomorrow; for tomorrow shall take thought of the things of itself. Sufficient unto the day is the evil thereof."
>
> —Matthew 6:34

> "Choose you this day whom ye will serve."
>
> —Joshua 24:15

Jesus said, "Take no thought for tomorrow." Why? You may never see tomorrow, and even if you do, you never know what the day may bring. You have no control over tomorrow. When you set goals to achieve something in the future, you tend to focus on a time not yet come and that you may never see. Instead, set your goals with the view that they have already been achieved and that each day you are living the life you have imagined.

Setting goals for some future time and living in the present may seem contradictory. Remember the story about actor/comedian Jim Carrey? He wrote himself a check for $10 million and it was dated ten years in the future. In the meantime, every day, Jim Carrey would venture off into his imagination, and in his mind, he lived the life that he was expecting. This is precisely what I mean by living your future life now. Living with expectancy will eventually produce the life you have imagined.

Goal setting helps you put your vision to paper, which gives your subconscious mind a clearer picture of what your new life is supposed to look like. Have you ever noticed that, once your subconscious mind has a clear picture of what it is that you want, doors begin to open and opportunities just seem to drop in your lap? Believe it or not, those opportunities have always been right where you are. The difference is, you have grown to the point of recognizing those that you could not see before.

"What is the most effective thing I can do right now: That will lead me to my goals, my vision, and my purpose."

—Herbert Harris

Each day of your life, choose to transform your thinking towards a higher level of growth. The things coming into your life now are much different than the things you were receiving in your earlier stages. As you mature and develop, revelations come a lot quicker and more often. There seem to be more opportunities coming your way. Don't prepare tomorrow for what is available to you today.

Many opportunities become available to you depending on the development of your own thinking. At some point, you grow into the level of your success. A multi-millionaire is not born with the knowledge to become a multi-millionaire. That person has done years of self-development that eventually allowed them to elevate their thinking and their self-worth. Opportunity follows you wherever you go. It is always there. Either you have grown to a place where you can recognize the opportunities around you, or you will walk right alongside of them never noticing who or what they are.

Everything that you receive in life is predicated upon your being prepared for it. Whether you are or whether you're not prepared, it doesn't really matter in the scheme of things, because either you will be ready to receive it, or you will be helping to prepare it for someone else to receive. Either way, someone will recognize and take hold of opportunity.

The five Ps of success are "Proper Preparation Prevents Poor Performance." When you have grown yourself to the point of living a life of excellence, you will find that opportunities will be made available even when you're not looking. It is much easier to operate in the spirit of excellence moment by moment as opposed to thinking about doing it an entire lifetime.

Practice doing things to the best of your ability in segments of moments. Concentrate on actively doing, listening and speaking in *this* moment, *right now*! Don't let your mind wander off into some future or dwell on some past event; instead, give your undivided attention to whomever or whatever you are doing *now*!

If you are giving a speech, don't focus on the number of people in the crowd or whether you're adequately touching every point; just relax and speak what you know with confidence and the expectation that all is going as it is supposed to. If you are having a conversation with someone, actively respond to give them the assurance that you are involved and attentive to what they are saying. They are spending time with you by choice, so don't waste their valuable time by mentally being somewhere else. Every moment that someone else allots to you, they are extending knowledge and resources as an investment in you. It was by divine appointment that you connected, and there is a divine reason and purpose for it all to be happening right now.

If you learn to flow with life, it will continue to connect the dots leading towards your destiny. When you think in terms of the moment that you're in, there are so many more things that you can do well. I can say a kind word in a moment's time. I can put a radiant smile across my face. I can listen intently and show compassion. I can choose to operate in a spirit of excellence or give away myself for their benefit. I can control so much more in a moment than I can the rest of my life, especially since I do not know how long the rest of my life is or what my future holds for me. All of that is totally outside my control, but what I do in the moment that I am in is completely in my control.

Joy, happiness, success and character are not things that you are born into. You don't come out of your mother's womb with any understanding or knowledge about life or how to live it. You have no understanding about principles, relationships or how to get the things you want in life. All these things happen with personal growth, which means that you or someone else has to pour into your life. Most of us did not end up where we are all by ourselves. Someone mentored us or pointed us in the right direction, gave us a gift that changed our perspective. Those who have achieved great success had a helping hand somewhere from someone. Whether it was a gentle push, a shining example or a life-changing discussion, someone thought it worth their time, their knowledge or their resources to set you on your way.

"It is literally true that you can succeed best and quickest by helping others to succeed."

—Napoleon Hill

"A leader's job is not to do the work for others; it's to help others figure out how to do it for themselves, to get things done and to succeed beyond what they thought possible."

—Simon Sinok

"Success brings a measure of credibility. The fastest way to turn credibility into authority is to deliver results. The best way to deliver results is to help others succeed. You can help others succeed by being helpful.

Always look for ways to be helpful. Helpful people are always in demand."

—Richie Norton

Whatever single accomplishment that you have had in life, whether it be of great significance or of little consequence, always remember that we are to use our talents and abilities to serve others. Our purpose here on earth is not self-serving, but it is for the advancement and development of other human beings. We are not to challenge ourselves to get all we can get, but rather to give all that we can give. Sowing and reaping work the same in every avenue of life. It doesn't matter what it is—money, romance, popularity or success. It all happens much more quickly when your sole purpose is to elevate others. Never knock someone who is down on their luck; instead, reach out your hand with the intention of pulling them back up. At some point in your life, where they are, you have been. Remember, just because you came out of your mess, it doesn't give you the right to judge someone who hasn't made it out of theirs.

What we think about someone else's progress has no bearing on our own status. Diminishing someone else's position in life doesn't put you in a better place. Your being established is not based on your comparison with other people. You may have a better paying job, higher social status, far more education and better advantages, but if your character is flawed, then everything in your life is flawed. How you earn a living is flawed. Your family relationships are flawed. Your perspective about life and success are all flawed.

Your character determines every other aspect of your life. Poor character, poor life; great character, great life. Money has nothing to do with living a happy life. You can have millions and live with the fear of being killed every minute of every day because of how you earn those millions.

Peace of mind is the greatest treasure that any person could have. Sleeping at night without fear or worry would be ideal for most of us. Living in the present and assessing what is going on in the moment keeps you grounded. It also helps you see the opportunities that are available to you right now. Most of you who are missing opportunities are looking either into the future or examining your past overlooking what is present. Living in the present transitions you into a possibility thinker.

In the book *The 15 Invaluable Laws of Growth*, there is a story about a chicken farmer whose land flooded nearly every spring. He didn't want to give up his farm and move, but when the water backed up onto his land and flooded his chicken coops, it was always a struggle to get his chickens to higher ground. Some years he couldn't move fast enough, and some of his chickens drowned.

One year, after experiencing the worst spring ever and losing his entire flock, he came into the farmhouse and told his wife, "I have had it. I can't afford to buy another place. I can't sell this one. I don't know what to do."

His wife replied, "Buy ducks."

People who make the most of a bad experience are the ones who find creative ways to overcome them, like the farmer's wife in the story. They see possibilities within their problems. They see what opportunities are available to them *now*!

> "I believe it is a normal human desire to be concerned about how we look on the outside. There's nothing wrong with that. What can get us in trouble is worrying more about how we look on the outside than about how we really are on the inside."

—John C. Maxwell

Outward appearances don't always give an accurate depiction of what's going on inwardly. You can dress things up on the outside and carry malicious motives on the inside, and not move an inch closer to success. Until you clean up the inside, you will never have success of any great magnitude.

> "Winning in life is more than just money . . . it's about winning on the inside . . . and knowing that you have played the game of life with all you had . . . and then some."

—Doug Firebaugh

Two people can live the exact same life experiences and still end up taking totally different paths. In her book *Choose the Happiness Habit*, Pam Golden tells a story of two siblings reared in the same home with the same parents. She writes, "Take the story of two brothers who were twins. One grows up to be an alcoholic bum. The other becomes an extremely successful businessman. When the alcoholic is asked why he became a drunk, he replies,

'My father was a drunk.' When the successful businessman is asked why he became successful, he says, 'My father was a drunk.' Same background. Same upbringing. Very different choices."

The brothers had an identical experience, and yet, they chose different thoughts and, over time, produced completely opposite circumstances.

Whatever thoughts are held in our minds consistently eventually formulate habits that become our lifestyle. Those who look at hurdles and hardships as a form of bad luck just attract more of the same. Ever hear of Murphy's Law "Anything that can go wrong will go wrong."? When you live in the illusion of expecting things to go awry, trust me, they will.

Years ago, I was in the Army. I was stationed at Fort Lewis, Washington. It rained a lot there. Most people vehemently complained about not being able to enjoy the outdoors because it was always drizzling or pouring. People would say, "It's rainy and gloomy outside. I love the outdoors. Why does it have to rain so much?" They would reluctantly pull out their umbrellas, murmuring while walking out to their cars. I had a totally different outlook about rainy days. Since we had to be indoors anyway, I got a lot of handy work done around the house. There were plenty of indoor activities. We could play pool, go bowling, check out a movie, go roller skating or curl up with a good book. Everything is about perspective.

Torrential rains always gave our platoon sergeant an opportunity to assign us indoor maintenance and clean-up. There was always tons of work to do at the motor pool during the rainy season.

There were parts to clean and repair. There was a lot of painting to be done. We had regulatory safety schematics that had to be updated and modified.

The military had a saying that we all had to adhere to: "There is a place for everything and everything in its place." All of the tools that hung on the peg boards had to have an outline drawn of that specific tool so that anyone could find and put that tool in its proper place. Everything we did was what we used to call "dress right, dress." Our gig lines had to be perfectly straight, which is where the button seam of your shirt had to line up with your trouser seam near your belt buckle. So the rainy season never stopped the Army from finding something productive for us to do. Boredom was never an issue.

One of the key lessons I learned while in the military was how to respond to what was happening in the moment. Being a young soldier and coming from an impoverished neighborhood in the Jim Crow South had imprinted so many psychological limitations in my mind that my living in the moment always consisted of surviving, but never really living and experiencing the significance of that moment. In order to live in the present moment, your mind must be clear of all other distractions. Worry, fear, uncertainty and doubt will prevent you from focusing on what is right in front of you. It will obliterate your ability to concentrate and be aware of your true reality in that moment.

Self-development grows you to the point that worry, fear, uncertainty and doubt no longer affect your ability to focus in the present moment. Your future depends on how you respond to what is happening in this moment.

Have you ever heard a person say, "One day when I am rich, I am travelling all over the world." What does being rich have to do with your being able to travel? The reality is that most people who are travelling are not rich, and yet, they manage to travel extensively. Why? Because their "someday" is now, and that's where they are living.

Any time you talk about someday, you are deciding at that moment to live in a future that you don't have. Someday is not your life. Today, right now is your life. All you can do is think about what happened in the past or imagine what could happen in the future, or decide to live right where you are with whatever you have.

You only have the power to adapt to whatever is happening in the present moment. You can't rectify what's happened in the past, and you can't foresee the future. You can imagine the future and how you'd like to see your life unfold. You can dwell on the past and relive those things that have happened, good or bad; however, none of that gives you an advantage right now.

The comprehension of living your future now may not come easy for some. The question is, why imagine a future that you may not ever see? Because life's journey is full of possibilities, and there is a possibility that you might live to be 120 years old. If that is the case, somewhere along the line, you had to put a plan in place just in case.

There is absolutely nothing wrong in planning your future. Whatever future you have designed for yourself must come with the understanding that it may or may not happen and, either way, that's okay. Once you relinquish the story about knowing your future, you can accept living in the moment. Only God knows the beginning and the end.

> "Therefore I say unto you, what things soever ye desire, when ye pray, believe that ye receive them, and ye shall have them."
>
> —Mark 11:24 (KJV)

The Bible clearly states that, whatsoever you desire, when you pray (speak), believe that you receive them and you shall have them. In my mind's eye, I have seen (desired). I have prayed (spoken). I believe (faith). I already have them. To live the life you have envisioned, you must possess a powerful and vivid imagination.

The secret is to learn how to pull your future into the present using your five physical senses of sight, touch, smell, taste and hearing along with imagination. One of the most effective ways to utilize your imagination is to find a quiet, dark room or location where you will be uninterrupted. Follow these simple but effective steps below. This exercise will be challenging for you initially, but continue anyway.

1. *Take ten deep breaths, and get your body in a relaxed state.*

2. *Focus on your breathing in and out.*

3. *Listen to your heartbeat as your lungs inflate and deflate.*

4. *Get in tune with your five senses.*

5. *Now picture in your mind those things you desire or whatever problems that you are struggling with and that you need answers to.*

6. *Once the vision has come into view, hold it there and concentrate on what is going on in that picture. Bring as much into focus as possible.*

7. *See yourself doing or being whatever it is that you have imagined. Experience the sights, smells, tastes, sounds and noises.*

8. *Live right there in that vision as long as you can.*

This will leave a very deep and lasting imprint upon your subconscious mind. Do this daily first thing in the morning if possible, and make this the last thing you do at nighttime right before going to sleep. This exercise done consistently over time will dramatically change your life.

You will start finding it easier and easier to do the things that you are supposed to. You will begin to attract everything necessary to make that vision materialize in your life. The things you once struggled with will start diminishing, and what you are supposed to do, you will do. Imagery properly used can expeditiously turn your vision into your reality.

CHAPTER TWELVE

Imagination Manifests Desires

D reamers have always understood the power of imagination. The world we live in today is a very different place because of those who have brought to life their remarkable ideas. Many of the people who have dramatically changed the world have been ostracized, ridiculed and alienated.

Thomas Edison's invention of the light bulb was considered unworthy by the scientific community when it was first introduced. His tenacity and unwavering desire have made our world a much brighter place.

Critics considered the automobile as impractical, and analysts believed that it would never be able to replace the bicycle. In 1899, *Literary Digest* stated, "The ordinary 'horseless carriage' is at present a luxury for the wealthy; and although its price will probably fall in the future, it will never, of course, come into as common use as the bicycle." Henry Ford ignored these criticisms and launched the mass production of the automobile, making it accessible to everyone. Today, automobiles rule the highways.

Western Union shrugged off the invention of the telephone, and it was totally disregarded as a toy. They refused to buy the rights to the patent for $100,000, so Alexander Graham Bell decided to establish the Bell Telephone Company and sold 1.5 million telephones the following year. He believed in his invention when no one else did.

These men were dreamers who saw a world that could be a better place because of their inventions. The advent of television created a dynamic that gave entertainers, athletes and news conglomerates access to the world stage. Now 1.5 billion homes across the globe have at least one television set.

Internet access has made our world a much smaller place and has had a huge impact on the way we communicate and conduct business. Ken Olson, founder of DEC Corporation, said, "There was no reason for anyone to want a computer in their home." Of course, this was back in 1977 when computers were the size of a living room. Inventor Charles Babbage, considered the father of the digital device or computer, would have never imagined his creation being the size of a cell phone. Today, you can communicate across the world with a device that fits in the palm of your hand.

All of these magnificent inventions came from the minds of those with extraordinary imaginations, people who were looking to make an impact on how we all live. Dreamers imagine things that stretch far beyond what the average person can see.

At no point throughout history has it been shown that people with big dreams and larger-than-life imaginations have ever been accepted by the status quo. Very seldom will people buy into what they don't understand. A dreamer doesn't see with the eyes of the flesh hoping for their idea to materialize. They see a clear vision with their mind's eye of a finished, working product serving all of mankind on a very large scale.

In the late 1800s, while many saw the bicycle as the next best thing, Henry Ford saw something far greater that would add a level of travel and convenience to mankind that no one else could fathom. His vision was inconceivable to everyone else but him, the dreamer.

It has been chronicled that Thomas Edison failed a thousand times before successfully inventing the light bulb; however, as the inventor, he never saw them as failures. All he could ever see was that he was getting closer to bringing his dream to realization. He could have had a recorded ten thousand failures, and it would not have prevented him from succeeding at delivering to the world what he saw in his vision.

Orville and Wilbur Wright imagined man safely travelling through the air in flight. There were crashes, mishaps and unforeseen forces that caused failure after failure. Those who have an end result in mind never see failure but stepping stones towards the achievement of their vision. On December 14, 1903, at 10:35

a.m., they had a successful flight that lasted 12 seconds and flew 120 feet. By the end of the day, they flew for nearly a minute for a distance of 852 feet. Today, we travel all over the world country to country as routinely as driving across town. Because of these two pioneers who refused to accept anything less than success, man has since set foot on the moon.

Now the possibilities are there to one day be able to explore other planets and solar systems. Dreamers make things happen that at first seem out of the ordinary to help create something extraordinary.

Albert Einstein is known as one of the greatest mathematicians of our time. One of his most famous quotes is, "I am enough of an artist to draw freely upon my imagination. Imagination is more important than knowledge. For knowledge is limited, whereas imagination encircles the world." He considered the ability to draw upon his imagination as that of an artist.

Men are limited by what they can think, but the imagination is not bound by the same limitations. The imagination is a master workshop and an unlimited source of ideas, inventions, concepts and creations. It is a vast ocean filled with endless possibilities of anything conceivable by the mind of man. Anything that can be imagined can be created. There is no problem that can't be solved with our imaginations.

In his book *Think and Grow Rich*, Napoleon Hill describes two types of imagination: synthetic imagination and creative imagination. This is what he says:

"Synthetic Imagination

Through this faculty, one may arrange old concepts, ideas, or plans into new combinations. This faculty creates nothing. It merely works with the material of experiences, education, and observation with which it is fed. It is the faculty used most by the inventor, with the exception of the 'genius' who draws upon the creative imagination when he cannot solve his problem through synthetic imagination.

. . .

Creative Imagination

Through the faculty of creative imagination, the finite mind of man has direct communication with Infinite Intelligence. It is the faculty through which 'hunches' and 'inspirations' are received. It is by this faculty that all basic or new ideas are handed over to man. It is through this faculty that thought vibrations from the minds of others are received. It is through this faculty that one individual may 'tune in' or communicate with the subconscious minds of other men."

—Napoleon Hill

Our creative imagination is working for us continuously. The thoughts we consistently hold in our conscious mind sooner or later trigger the emotion of burning desire. This desire ignites the working power of the subconscious mind. Desire is simply a thought. It floats into your mind in an instant, and disappears just as quickly.

It is there long enough to plant a seed. That seed is cultivated and nurtured until it is transformed into its physical equivalent.

Like any muscle, imagination becomes weak without use. It never goes away or becomes inactive. When you go to the gym on a regular basis, and your muscles become accustomed to a workout regimen, you no longer experience the deep soreness as when you began. Then you don't go to the gym for five maybe six months. You go in, you work out and you wake up the next day barely able to get out of bed. You are sore from head to toe. You can hardly walk across the floor because your legs both feel like mush, and the pain of walking across the floor is unbearable.

Eventually the pain subsides, and your workouts are so much easier. Your imagination is the same way. The more you exercise it, the more alert and responsive it becomes. Over time, it will get to a point that you can see clear, vivid pictures of anything you desire. Most highly successful people have first imagined themselves being what they eventually become. They have played out their lives in their imagination over and over until it became a living, breathing manifestation. It was a reality they were living in their minds long before it materialized.

Every fortune ever made began with an idea initiated by a single thought. In his book *Think and Grow Rich*, Napoleon Hill tells a story about an enchanted kettle. The story is relevant as an example of this concept about a single thought coupled with imagination being able to amass a fortune.

Fifty years ago, an old country doctor drove to town, hitched his horse, quietly slipped into a drugstore by the back door and began "dickering" with a young drug clerk.

His mission was destined to yield great wealth to many people. It was destined to bring to the South the most far-flung benefit since the Civil War.

For more than an hour, behind the prescription counter, the old doctor and the clerk talked in low tones. Then the doctor left. He went out to the buggy and brought back a large, old-fashioned kettle and a big wooden paddle (used for stirring the contents of the kettle), and deposited them in the back of the store.

The clerk inspected the kettle, reached into his inside pocket, took out a roll of bills and handed it over to the doctor. The roll contained exactly $500—the clerk's entire savings!

The doctor handed over a small slip of paper on which was written a secret formula. The words on that small slip of paper were worth a king's ransom! But not to the doctor. Those magic words were needed to start the kettle to boiling. But neither the doctor nor the young clerk knew what fabulous fortunes were destined to flow from that kettle.

The old doctor was glad to sell the outfit for the five-hundred dollars. The money would pay off his debts, and give him freedom of mind. The clerk was taking a big chance by staking his entire life's savings on a mere scrap of paper and an old kettle. He never dreamed his investment would start a kettle to overflow with gold that would surpass the miraculous performance of Aladdin's lamp.

What the clerk really purchased was an idea.

The old kettle and the wooden paddle and the secret message on the slip of paper were incidental. The strange performance of the kettle began to take place after the new owner mixed with the secret instructions an ingredient of which the doctor knew nothing.

This idea has produced vast fortunes of gold. It has paid, and still pays, huge fortunes to men and women all over the world who distribute the contents of the kettle to millions of people.

The old kettle is now one of the world's largest producers of sugar, thus providing jobs of a permanent nature to thousands of men and women engaged in growing sugarcane and in refining and marketing sugar:

- The Enchanted Kettle consumes, annually, millions of glass bottles, providing jobs to huge numbers of glass workers.

- The Enchanted Kettle gives employment to an army of clerks, stenographers, copywriters and advertising experts throughout the nation. It has brought fame and fortune to scores of artists who have created magnificent pictures describing the product.

- The Enchanted Kettle has converted a small Southern city into the business capital of the South, where it now benefits, directly or indirectly, every business and practically every resident in the city.

The influence of this idea now benefits every civilized country in the world, pouring out a continuous stream of gold to all who touch it.

All through the world depression, when factories, banks and business houses were folding up and quitting by the thousands, the owner of The Enchanted Kettle went marching on, giving continuous employment to an army of men and women all over the world, and paying extra portions of gold to those who, long ago, had faith in the idea.

Whoever you are, wherever you may live, whatever occupation you may be engaged in, just remember in the future that, every time you see the words "Coca-Cola," its vast empire of wealth and influence grew out of a single idea, and that the mysterious ingredient the drug clerk—Asa Candler—mixed with the secret formula was . . . imagination!

Now think about this story that Napoleon Hill described here. There was a doctor who had an amazing formula that he happily sold for $500. He left the agreement in a good place. He ended up debt free, and yet he lacked just one ingredient that would have made him a fortune of a lifetime—imagination!

Somewhere along our life's journey, we forgot how to use our imagination. Maybe as we matured, it seemed silly to pretend to be something that we weren't. It is possible that we felt foolish or childish delving off into a world of make-believe and fantasy.

The highly successful have not relinquished this precious jewel. They have learned the art of thinking upon the things that they want, realizing that ideas will eventually stem from those thoughts. They use the conscious mind like the guard at the palace deciding which thoughts get in and which ones don't. They carry with them an elaborate guest list of thoughts of their choosing, deciding with great intentionality and consistently their insertion day in and day out.

Once ideas begin to flow from those thoughts, they are written down on paper to be reviewed on a regular basis. Constant review does a couple of things: it gives the mind a clear picture of what it is that you want, and it fuels the imagination. That clear and present idea coupled with imagination creates its physical equivalent. This is the exact same process that you can use to have everything that you desire in life.

The idea of a happy marriage or a loving relationship starts with the thought of wanting a happy marriage or a loving relationship. Being healthy and physically fit begins with the thought of seeing yourself that way. Earning wealth and abundance, having overflow and living a life of abundance all begin with a thought. Many of us have heard the analogy that thoughts become things. I would like to add that continuous thoughts that formulate ideas coupled with imagination eventually become things.

Why did I frame it up this way? Nothing gets completed by just having the thought. If that was the case, every single person that you met would at least be a millionaire. Most people's expectations are much higher than the life they are living. If you were to ask a hundred people if they'd like to be rich, most likely you would get ninety-nine "yeses" and one "maybe." There is always one that will take the opposite approach no matter what. So if just the thought itself created wealth, there would be no working poor. Thought has to grow into some type of an idea. It's the idea that creates the leverage needed to get your imagination involved. Now once those two harmonize together, whatever you desire, you will have!

Why do so many fail to understand the simple method of inserting the right thoughts into their own minds on a consistent basis? Most people will never do what they were never taught. A vast majority of people walk around with no clue how to get their most basic desires fulfilled. It is not taught at any level of schooling. It is not taught in the majority of homes across the world. No one is making neighborhood visits door to door handing this knowledge out to everyone. People just don't know.

People for the most part don't seek the right information. After all, it is accessible. With the advent of the Internet, computers, iPads and cell phones, information is at our beck and call twenty-four hours a day seven days a week.

The self-help industry sold $9.9 billion worth of products in 2016. So what seems to prevent people from having what they desire? Obviously, the thought of obtaining a better life is very popular. Unfortunately, reading about it is not enough. You can read a thousand books in your lifetime and never change a single thing about your life. It is not the reading of books. It is not failing to have access. It is not that the information is bad or incorrect. Thoughts without intentionality are just fleeting impulses that fly into the mind only to exit just as quickly as they came.

Fleeting thoughts have zero impact on improving your life. Until you learn the value of action and consistency, your reality will not improve. Imagination is a very powerful tool and, just like working out at the gym, requires you to not only get there, but do something when you do. Thinking about working out will never get the results that you seek. You can spend eighteen hours a day thinking about going to the gym, but until you get there with the intention to do the work, it's just a fleeting thought.

Fleeting thoughts will never trigger the awesome power of your imagination. A fleeting thought will never live in your mind long enough to formulate an idea. Since an idea is what ignites and then fuels the imagination, if not tapped into, it will lay dormant. It won't be persuaded to wake up or perform without the nudging of an idea. It will become weaker over time, offering its host zero benefit.

Imagination can take you from the world that you are currently in to an ideal world in the blink of an eye. It can paint a different mental image from a depressed, destitute state to a joyful, empowering state. Imagination operates beyond just our five senses. Imagination has the ability to create mental images that are not perceived by sight, taste, touch, hearing or smell. Our imagination can create a future that we have never been exposed to or bring something from the past to the present. It can reconstruct our lives from the ground up in an instant.

Every living soul on earth has imaginative capabilities. Some are more adept at using their imaginations, while others have little to no experience. Imagination becomes more developed with use and weakens with inactivity. Developing your imagination can literally change your life. Imagination opens up possibilities to you and allows you to experience whole new worlds inside your mind. It lets you see life's situations in different perspectives and can examine the past and the future.

Imagination has no limitations. It will give you whatever your mind is capable of conceiving. Imagination is not relegated to only using imagery to create. It also uses your five senses, your emotions, your past and your innermost desires to orchestrate new worlds. It is the only tool that we possess that can take us out of a life of chaos into a world of serenity and order any time we choose. There is no rationing of our imaginations. We have no quota or limited time to use it. Our imaginations are available to us twenty-four hours a day every day of the week.

"But as it is written, Eye hath not seen, nor ear heard, neither have entered into the heart of man, the things which God hath prepared for them that love him."

—1 Corinthians 2:9

"O LORD God of Abraham, Isaac, and of Israel, our fathers, keep this forever in the imagination of the thoughts of the heart of thy people, and prepare their heart unto thee."

—1 Chronicles 29:18

Imagination is the most powerful and effective resource we have to bring about instant manifestation. There is a well-known story of a young preacher by the name of Frank W. Gunsaulus. He was a masterful orator who captivated the wealthy and influential with dazzling sermons from his pulpit at Plymouth Church located in Chicago, Illinois. He is best recognized for his unforgettable "Million Dollar Sermon." He often preached to some of the most prominent people of that era like George Pullman, a railroad magnate, and Marshall Field, owner of Marshall Field & Company.

In 1890, he delivered a sermon for the ages while a man by the name of Philip D. Armour was in attendance. His sermons were usually centered around the wealthy's social responsibility to those less fortunate. On this particular day, he painted a picture in the minds of those in attendance of what he would do if he had a million dollars. He talked about how he would start a school to help the younger generation train for jobs in the new industrial age.

During Dr. Gunsaulus' college years, he noticed that the educational system was ineffective and believed that he could provide a better system of learning and education if he were running the institution. After much thought, he made the decision to organize a new college and implement his ideas without being crippled by conventional institutional processes. In order to carry out his plan, he needed a million dollars. He did not have this kind of money.

Two years went by without any real progress. One day, while milling in his mind ways to raise the money he needed, he realized that he had done nothing but think. He decided that he had done enough thinking and that it was time to take action. He made a declaration that he would get the money within a week.

Next, he contacted the local newspaper and placed an announcement that the following morning he would preach a sermon entitled "What I Would Do if I Had a Million Dollars." He woke up the next morning early, read over his sermon in the bathroom, then knelt down on his knees and prayed that his sermon would motivate someone to contribute the million dollars.

He walked up to the pulpit and began his sermon. He shared his dreams with passion and enthusiasm. He explained what he would do if he had someone place that amount of money in his hands. He described details about how he would organize a great educational institution teaching young people practical skills while at the same time developing their minds.

At the completion of his sermon, a man slowly rose up from his seat and began to make his way towards the pulpit. As he approached Dr. Gunsaulus, he extended his hand and said, "Reverend, I liked your sermon. I believe you can do everything you that you said if you had a million dollars. My name is Philip D. Armour."

Dr. Gunsaulus was invited to Mr. Armour's office where he was given a check for one million dollars. With that million dollars, he founded the Armour Institute of Technology. The institution's name has since been changed to Illinois Institute of Technology.

Imagination gave Dr. Gunsaulus access to resources that were normally unavailable to him. He held thoughts for years about implementing a better system of education, and yet, it was imagination that evoked actions that finally presented the right opportunity at the perfect moment in time.

He painted a picture of developing the next generation while also providing resources for the future growth and expansion of the industrial revolution. He recognized the needs of those having to prepare to enter the new world of industry and those who were creating the industry. He provided an idea of a system that would benefit everyone, including his own aspirations.

There are millions of people around the world hoping that someone would write them a $1,000,000 check. Imagination is bigger than hope. Imagination stems from an idea, and an idea engages the minds and hearts of those who hear it. Imagination could be construed as man's greatest cerebral attribute. However, imagination, once unhinged from wisdom, can become our biggest vulnerability. The same capability to devise and invent is also what can draw us away from a reality that's been established by practical application and prudence.

Everything we do can have a positive or negative outcome. Imagination is no different. When we use our imagination to create the things we desire, and have goals and action steps for its achievement, this is the positive side of imagination.

Then there is the negative aspect, which is living in the fantasy of another life with no clear vision, goals or action steps to make it a reality. Two very distinct perceptions with very different approaches. Really, there are only two types of people: those who get things accomplished, and those who don't. A determined person who is focused and accustomed to taking action to make things happen will get results, and then there are those who imagine without little to no expectation of manifesting what they see in their minds. The person that takes action is doing the things necessary to make their dream a reality, whereas some live in their imagination to get relief from a miserable existence.

Imagination can wield the power to bring a whole new world into existence, or leave a person stuck in a low and debilitating state. The proper use of imagination can bring excitement, joy and a strong sense of accomplishment. The evidence of how you're using your imagination shows up in your everyday life. Those who are progressing in knowledge, wisdom and prosperity are experiencing what they have created from their imaginations, while those living in despair, lack and impracticality are using their imaginations to escape.

Whether you're using your imagination for transformation or to shield yourself from reality, it will provide you exactly what you expect it to. One of the best habits that a person can adapt is the habit of action. A dream is but a dream until it is written down on paper followed with goals and action steps for its attainment.

This habit of action solves a lot of problems we face in life. Procrastination and slothfulness are the enemies of progression. A dream living in your mind will stay there forever, always longing to become a reality. If you do not do the things that you must do to have those things that you have imagined, you're using one of the most powerful tools known to man to simply escape the world you do not want to face. Imagination can have no bearing on changing your reality until you employ the habit of action. I can't stress enough the importance of developing habits that help you realize your dreams.

Examine the real you, and face your shortcomings. Once you have identified those things that are keeping you stuck, access every tool available to you that will help you develop habits that transform you. The very first place to start is by practicing to use words effectively. Words will train your thoughts and nourish your imagination to do remarkable things in your life.

CHAPTER THIRTEEN

Master Your Words

Words are the cornerstone for the life we build. The most critical component of any structure is its foundation. A building can't stand the test of time without a solid foundation; the elements will sooner or later destroy it. Words are the building blocks to a healthy, joyful and prosperous life, and therefore, we must learn to choose them wisely.

Words are responsible for every aspect of our lives. Every word we speak comes with enormous consequences. If we can just resolve in our minds that each word we let roll off our tongues is a gold nugget, and each one of those words is placed in a storehouse called our subconscious minds, then the storehouse begins to grow in size and in wealth.

As it begins to overflow, it has to start investing so that it can make room for more gold nuggets. It begins to formulate ideas and strategies that transform into the reality you have imagined. The fruit of your labor begins to pay off with the manifestation of many of those things that you have desired. Your gold nuggets have ignited your imagination to expand to the size of your vision. Things are now happening at a pace that you could have never imagined.

Wealth and abundance are flowing in from all directions. The key to what you are now experiencing has always been your words. Once we clearly understand the significance of what we say and the effect those words have on our lives, we will treat each and every word like a gold nugget. We will see each one as an investment sprinkled across the canvas of our imagination providing to us amazing ideas, inventions and opportunities.

A word is much more than a verb, adverb, noun or pronoun. Every word that you spew out of your mouth should have a purpose. Whether you attach a purpose to your words or not will not change the effect of what those words will do. They will accomplish exactly what was spoken.

There are only two outcomes that our words will create. Words will either create our desires, or they will create the opposite. There is no in-between or gray area. Your words will create a positive result or a negative result. Speaking the life that you want must be done with intention.

Master your thoughts and rule your tongue, and the things that you desire will come into your life. We are made in the image of God after His likeness and endowed with His attributes.

"For as the rain cometh down, and the snow from heaven, and returneth not thither, but watereth the earth

and maketh it bring forth and bud, that it may give seed
to the sower and bread to the eater. So shall my word be
that goeth forth out of my mouth: it shall not return unto
me void, but it shall accomplish that which I please, and
it shall prosper in the thing whereto I sent it."

—Isaiah 55:10-11 KJV

God's Word waters everything that it touches, and it gives
seed to the sower and bread to the eater. It shall not return unto me
void and it shall accomplish and it shall prosper. I actually get goose
bumps when I really think about the significance of these verses and
how it applies to us as spirit beings having the attributes of God.
Our words then are designed to water or give life to all that they
come into contact with.

Once we release our word, it will go forth and be sown in some
to share with others and it will enter into the heart of some who
are ready for it. Our words will not return unto us void, and they
will accomplish those things that we please and they shall prosper
where into we send them.

Our words work the same way that God's Word works. "And
the LORD God formed man of the dust of the ground, and breathed
into his nostrils the breath of life; and man became a living soul."
When He breathed into his nostrils the breath of life, He passed
along His attributes and with that came the power to create with
our words.

God created everything on this earth that we experience by
speaking it into existence. Now that I know that whatever I speak

shall not return unto me void and that my words will accomplish whatever I please and that they will prosper wherever I send them, it makes me realize that whatever battle rages within me to control what I think, how I feel and what I say is worth every ounce of energy to ensure that I think the right things, that I feel how I should and that I say only those things that I want in my life. If I want joy, I must think, believe and speak joy. If I want happiness, then I must choose happiness. If I want wealth, then I must desire to be wealthy. We have the ability to control every single aspect of our lives simply by understanding and developing enough discipline to control the things we think, how we want to feel and the words spewing out of our mouths.

God has put in us the ability to control our own destinies by applying these simple principles. Why is something so simple so difficult for many of us to do? Most of us were born into and reared in the world system. We were not taught Kingdom principles. We had no idea who we were or what our capabilities were because those responsible, in most cases, did not seek or know anything about God.

Some were fortunate enough to be raised in a Godly home under the guidance of two parents that loved God and instilled His principles from the time of birth. However, this is far from the normal household. Most households scattered across the world have absolutely no clue about who they are. The cold, harsh reality is that the world has gotten as far away from God as possible.

Prayer has been removed from the school system, the Ten Commandments are no longer a standard that society lives by and the workplaces across the United States barely allow the mention of Jesus or any holidays associated with the Risen Savior.

We live in a society that doesn't want God as part of their everyday lives except when they need him. Then there is a cry for prayer and solidarity. God is not just a crisis God. He is the one and only living God. With Him all things are possible, and when we choose God, we choose to live in power and the expectation of great and mighty things. God is our source and provider. Every night this is one of the statements I read right before I fall off to sleep.

> "I am now writing in my subconscious mind the idea of Gods wealth. God is the source of my supply and God is the life principle within me and I know that I am alive and all my needs are met in every moment of time and every point of space. God's wealth flows freely, joyously and ceaselessly in my experience and I give thanks for God's riches forever circulating in my experience."
>
> —Joseph Murphy

This is a very powerful statement to recite right before bedtime. This is speaking into your life with intent. If we carefully choose what we say to ourselves, about ourselves and within ourselves, transformation will inevitably happen.

There is a collection of other statements that I say right before sleeping at night and as soon as I wake up in the morning. I do this diligently and with intent now that I know the effect of what I say and think right before sleep is imperative to shaping who I want to become.

The subconscious mind never stops working, so the things that we input into it right before sleep gives it something positive to work with and create from while resting. This is not something that you do for a few days or even just a few weeks. This is something that is now a lifestyle. It doesn't have to be the same statement or statements for life, but the task of inputting positive information into your subconscious mind right before sleep is key. Since the subconscious mind is 95 percent of your brain function, deciding what happens there is one of the most crucial aspects for internal development and growth.

Have you ever seen a picture with the tip of an iceberg barely pecking above the water and the rest of the iceberg underwater is this vast, humungous piece with the appearance of a huge mountain? That picture is supposed to be representing 5 percent of the iceberg above the ocean and the other 95 percent below the water unseen. Now visualize that 5 percent being your conscious mind and the 95 percent beneath the water is your subconscious mind.

This picture is a perfect illustration of your brain. The 5 percent you can see and control are the words you speak, the things you allow into your eye gate, what you listen to or hear and what you taste, touch or smell. We have total control of most of those five senses. On the other hand, the 95 percent that you cannot see, feel, touch, hear or smell controls the real you.

This is the part of you that houses your fears, your habits and your traits. All of the things that make up who you have become are hidden here, in your subconscious mind. We have no idea what is really buried deep down in this thing we call the subconscious. All we can do is use the knowledge that we have accumulated to make dramatic change to that 95 percent as much as possible. When we learn how to invest in our subconscious, it will pay dramatic dividends in our lives.

We will have what we expect. Our subconscious knows exactly how to pull those things from the invisible to the physical. It will guide us to the right events, get us in touch with those who can help move us towards our vision and ignite in us a strong desire to finish what we have started. It will direct us on a course that will get us the swiftest results and the best possible choices. Your subconscious mind is the guidepost to a marvelous and successful life. Here is another statement that I say to myself right before I fall off asleep.

> "The old life is dead and buried. I have severed myself from it once and for all; henceforth, I live the new life of success and power of self-mastery and accomplishment. This I do not in the strength of my feeble will or surface of my consciousness but the infinite power of my deeper inner mind which is one with and forms a part of the infinite universal mind."
>
> —Ernest Holmes

The subconscious mind functions on repetition and emotion. You can instill any scenario that you want simply by being diligently repetitive about what you want changed deep down within you. Couple that with emotion, and you're on your way to a very new and different lifestyle. The question then that needs to be answered is, "How do I know what I have been subjected to and how much?" The only way to have any idea about what is housed in your subconscious mind is to take a long, hard look at what people that you personally know and respect had the largest impact on your child-rearing years on through your teenage years. Why is that relevant? Because whatever their core value system is was passed right along to you. Their perceptions about life were handed down to you. Their fears and limitations were automatically demonstrated to you over and over again until you developed those same fears. Where you lived and how you associated with others were most likely taught to you at a very early age. Well, before the ages of five or six, your personality had been created.

There is a lifetime of events stored in the archives of your subconscious mind. Everything that you've ever heard, touched, tasted, smelled or seen has been captured there. Every compliment as well as every criticism has been recorded. Every sensation has been felt, whether of pain or pleasure. Everything that's ever rolled across your palette in the way of fine cuisine or rock-gut, disgusting food not fit for a pig has never been forgotten. All that you have laid eyes upon, good or bad, has been registered in the subconscious mind. All of these sensations have created some kind of memories. Some have placed fears embedded deep down in your psyche. Some have raised your level of confidence, and some have left you in a state of limbo feeling hopeless and confused. In any case, everything and anything that you've ever experienced is available upon recall.

Imagine having a tool that has recorded every single thing pertaining to your life and will never forget. You may not be able to recall it, but it is still very accessible. Now think about the impact these experiences have had in shaping who you have become. There are things that you will not do because of some feeling or belief about it.

Let me cite a prime example from my own life. I am afraid of water and always have been. I never learned to swim and never had the desire to learn. My mother instilled this fear in all of us as young children. My mother never knew how to swim and was very afraid of water. She was so fearful of water that she never allowed any of us near it. Her fear became our fear, and we carried that fear all of our lives. Out of eight children, only one of us ever learned to swim and that was my middle brother. He taught himself by just jumping in the water and learning to doggie paddle. After getting accustomed to the water, he taught himself how to swim, and today, he is an excellent swimmer.

The words that I heard all my life were "Don't go near that water; you might drown." Those words impacted my life from that point on. My father was an excellent swimmer, but he did not help alleviate my fear of swimming one bit. He actually made it a lot worse.

One day he took us boys down to the public pool at Fifth Street Park. He decided to teach us all how to swim. His method was to toss each of us in the deep end of the pool and yell "Swim!" I flapped my arms and kicked my feet in a feeble attempt to do as my father had commanded, but the fear was overwhelming. I began to sink to the bottom of the pool. My dad had to jump in and bail me out.

The pool was full of people who all witnessed my horror that day. I was about eight years old then. I never even went near a pool again until I was about twenty-two years old. I was in the military at the time and was in a retraining brigade at Fort Riley, Kansas. One day, the drill sergeants got together and voted to take us all down to the pool. It was a sweltering hot day with high humidity, and we could hardly breathe or stay dry. We were all sweating profusely.

When we got to the pool, I could feel my anxiety level quickly rising. My pulse rate increased and my palms became sweaty from nervousness. I was so afraid that I felt like I was going to pass out. Deep down I wish I had, but I didn't. I was a soldier and I was not going to let the others see me limp on the ground passed out from fear. So I sucked it up, and got in line with the rest of the soldiers.

When it was my turn, the drill sergeant pushed me into the deep end of the pool. I had flashbacks of my dad doing the exact same thing, and the results were not good. Different person doing the pushing in a different location in a different year, and it was the exact same outcome. I sank to the bottom of the pool and the drill sergeant had to dive in and rescue me in front of all those men. I was so embarrassed that I could hardly look anyone in the eye. The drill sergeant called me a few choice names and ordered me to the barracks to dry off. I got teased the rest of the time there, and there wasn't anything I could do to live it down.

I have attempted to learn to swim a couple of other times in my life on my own, but the fear is still so overwhelming that, the moment the swim instructors try to challenge me to go to the deep end and swim, I have yet to overcome that barrier.

Words are very powerful and they have a lasting effect. I remember as a child we used to say, "Sticks and stones may break my bones but words will never harm me." That is by far one of the most untrue statements that I have ever heard.

Words cut down to the soul. They live deep down inside you cutting away at the very fiber of your being. I remember as a young boy, after my father left, my mother never had a good word to say about my dad. She used to get angry and tell me how much I was just like my no-good father and that I would never amount to anything. She would say, "You're just like your big-nose, pudgy daddy. You'll never amount to anything." I heard that more times than I care to think about. I never really thought about it back then. I just kind of shrugged it off to protect myself more than anything. As I got older, it seemed that, no matter what I tried in the way of a major achievement, I just never quite got to what I call that pinnacle of success, and I never really understood why.

Finally, after reading a book entitled *Unlimited Power* by Tony Robbins, I came to realize that I needed to do some deep, deep evaluation about who I was and how I came to be who I was.

I thought about my entire life from as far back as I could remember. What I began to clearly understand was that there were a lot of hurtful things said to me as a young child. I also experienced dire destitution, blatant racism, womanizing, lies, deceit and immorality.

I watched adults drink themselves into oblivion and act irresponsibly all because of poverty and self-pity. As far back as I can remember, I never heard any of the adults I was around ask, "How can I get beyond this?" "What can I do to change this situation?" "With where I am at right now, what are my options to turn my life around?" I never heard a single one of them ask the right questions. I heard questions like, "What am I am going to do?" "How do they expect me to come up with money I don't have?" "How do they expect us to survive on these wages?"

I truly believe that if you ask different questions, you will get better answers. Every problem has a solution, but in order to find the right one, you have to learn to ask better questions.

Some of the key questions that I asked myself during this in-depth evaluation were, "Who am I, and how did I become this way?" "What obstacles am I afraid to overcome?" "How come I am not successful in life? What is preventing me from having the things that I want?" "Why do I only get so far and never seem to get over the hump?" "Why do I continue to look outside myself for accountability of my own life?"

After meditating on these questions for days and then weeks, answers started floating into my mind. I began to see that I allowed my past experiences to carve out my future and that my present was a revamp of my past. I could not move forward in my life to the level that I was capable because I was stuck on all the things that were said and done in the past; it was impossible to create my new future.

I had to face my past and all the things that happened, and then let it all go. It was over. It no longer had a hold on me. Most of what happened was never true. It just seemed that way to an eleven-year-old kid who embraced all the anger, pity and self-destruction of those in my life.

It finally became clear that I had to develop a new vocabulary—one that spoke of life and abundance. I had to learn to increase my faith about what God had placed in me. I had to elevate my thought processes to a level of growth that would take me to a place I had never been.

I had always been right on the verge of success and never really understood what was holding me back. I was living in a past with a language that kept me there regardless of how hard I tried to move forward. If we want to create a better future, we must ask better questions and speak a different language. The language of success sounds and feels a lot different than the language of poverty. The Bible says to walk by faith, not by sight. If you live your life according to what you see, you will never have what you desire.

Your vision is far-reaching and extends way beyond what the physical eyes can see. Have you ever been around a person that is driven? I mean absolutely on fire for whatever it is that they are doing. It is because they have controlled their thoughts and have mastered their words. Can you imagine waking up every single day and only thinking about the things that you want in life? No negative thoughts being processed, nor doubt or unbelief, just an internal knowing that getting whatever you want is an option that you have if only you decide.

Not one single thing you do in life will ever be done without a clear decision to do it. Decision is the key that starts the engine. Once a decision has been made, a lot of other components begin to work together to move towards that decision. You must decide to create financial freedom. What makes it difficult to transition from financial deficiency to financial abundance is that you have said what you want without really believing that you will have it.

Mastering your words is more than just saying what you want. It is a combination of saying and feeling those things as though they were already present in your life. Feeling strongly about something creates belief. Our emotions are a huge part of our dynamic. They trigger our desires and stir up the passion necessary to fulfill our hopes and dreams. When used correctly, emotions can give us the drive that we need to get past an overwhelming obstacle or unexpected setback. How we think oftentimes will determine how we feel, and how we feel has a lot to do with what we say.

Have you ever observed someone who is down and out emotionally? Notice their language when they are expressing feelings of inadequacy, self-pity or delusion. Their demeanor matches what they are feeling, and what they are feeling is based on what they have been saying to themselves about their situation.

There are crossroads in every aspect of our lives. When we come to that fork in the road, we normally only have one of two options. You either go left or you go right. The thing is, life is full of forks in the road and you will always have to decide to take the left or the right. The right road or path, I should say, is usually pretty obvious. You're driving down a busy road, and you come to a light with the caution light on and it is about to turn red. You can choose to speed up and attempt to get past before the light turns red, or you can begin to press your brakes and stop.

If you do decide to run through the light, there are possible consequences. You could ram into an oncoming vehicle whose light just turned green. That crash into the side of that vehicle could cause you or someone else great bodily injury or death.

The other option would be to simply brake and stop at the light because a yellow light means caution. Poor thinking generally creates unfavorable circumstances. Unfavorable circumstances create depressing states that spur negative thinking, and the spiral just goes on and on. You must master your thoughts if you are ever going to master your words.

The words that come out of our mouths come from the heart, and what trickles down to the heart are the thoughts that we think. When we speak from the heart, we are speaking our truth. The truth that we speak has been created over time depending on our thoughts.

The thing is, once you begin to speak, the truth that you know has to come forth, because most of us can only speak what we know.

Now how did we come to know what we know? At some point, we thought these things that we are repeating. We put those thoughts there deep down in our hearts. So everything we say is based on what we have allowed ourselves to be taught. We allowed every single morsel of our heartfelt convictions to be placed there. Since we allowed it, we also have the power to remove it. No thought that we hold is immovable. We can decide to replace old thoughts with new ones anytime we choose.

We are ever evolving into something more, something greater, and at some point, we have to recognize that we do not operate at an earthly level. We are housed in an earthly body with a spiritual mind. That spiritual mind is the mind of God and knows all things.

We know exactly how to change the things in us that are not working. It is not a matter of not knowing' it is a matter of deciding to do what is necessary to make the change. Paying the price is what many of us avoid. I wish I was an Olympic champion in boxing. However, I don't like running 10 miles a day, me and jump roping don't mix, I really don't like bag work and, man, that medicine ball pounding on my stomach would be atrocious. This is the price to fulfill that wish so for many, all it will ever be is a wish.

It is the same thing with controlling our thoughts. There is a price. We must be intentional and diligent. We must be able to see that the outcome is well worth the effort. It takes an extreme amount of focus to stop and correct your thinking every single time you think a thought that does not serve you.

As time goes on, it gets easier and easier to hone in on what you are actually doing to yourself. We are blemishing our own minds with damaging thoughts that are driving us away from our purpose and not towards our purpose.

I really do believe that God puts in all of us a vision. The vision you obtain will be centered on your God-given ability. Whether we have identified what our talents and abilities are depends on our measure of self-observation. We must have an awareness of what we are naturally drawn to. What excites us? What do we respond to over and over again? What is it that we love so much that no one has to force us to do it? The things that you love to do are most likely your God-given abilities.

Get in the habit of speaking from a place of having rather than a place of lacking. If you are going to trick your subconscious mind into believing that you already have something, then let what you say reflect that. A good example is, "I am joyful, happy and energized." It doesn't matter whether I am feeling joyful, happy and energized; this is the feeling that I want, so this is what I am speaking. If I speak this long enough with conviction, then I will begin to feel this way.

Remember earlier that I mentioned only to speak those things that you want. Let's suppose I said, "I sure wish I could be happy, joyful and energized." There is no expectation to feel that way as per this sentence. Any sentence beginning with "I wish" or "I hope" are words that have no power. Nothing gets created in "I wish" or "I hope." They are not action words that produce any results. The words "I am" create the state you want to be in, and "I wish" is looking at some future time that you may not even have. There are two words that we should all remove from our vocabulary: wish and hope. I've never seen anything getting accomplished after wish or hope.

Every single word choice matters when it comes to creating your life. This is why it is so difficult for many to overcome a lot of the clichés that have been around for generations. This is why most are not producing the kind of lives that they are envisioning, because what they see and what they say do not match. If what you say and what you see do not match, it will not materialize. That is why it is imperative to learn different habits so that you can get better results.

Say what you mean, and mean what you say. If you say "I am going to wash the car in an hour," then get up and go wash the car in an hour. Don't get in the habit of saying one thing and doing another. This will not serve you in the long run. Every time you make a statement that you do not keep, it becomes a standard that you live by.

The inner man is torn because it operates from the spirit realm, which is of God, and God always does what He says. Now think about this for just a moment. You are causing a disruption in your Spirit Man by not keeping your word to yourself. When you make a claim of any type that is not true, you are ripping away at your own integrity.

When you are talking to anyone, you are talking to everyone, including yourself. Have you ever gotten upset and said a few choice words under your breath about someone else, usually while they were walking away? Those same words that you were directing at someone else were also heard by you; the emotion that you blurted that sentence out with is the same emotion that you gave unto yourself. This is why the Bible says to not judge.

> "Judge not, that ye be not judged. For with what judgment ye judge, ye shall be judged: and with what measure ye mete, it shall be measured to you again. And why beholdest thou the mote that is in thy brother's eye, but considerest not the beam that is in thine own eye? Or how wilt thou say to thy brother, 'Let me pull out the mote out of thine eye'; and, behold, a beam is in thine own eye? Thou hypocrite, first cast out the beam out of thine own eye; and then shalt thou see clearly to cast out the mote out of thy brother's eye."
>
> —Matthew 7:1-5

What do we normally judge with? Our words? Every thought we think and every word that we speak, we think and speak to ourselves. We must be careful about what we say and the intent behind what we say. It affects us all: those you are directing it towards and the person that's speaking them. We can't escape what we say, and our subconscious mind will never forget it. This is why God says to love thy neighbor as thyself, because what you speak against thy neighbor is also spoken against thyself. If you love your neighbor as yourself, you won't speak ill of them or yourself. This is the overwhelming reality and power of our words. We should only speak those things that we expect, and we should always be expecting good and marvelous things to happen in our lives.

What we expect is what we will receive. The things that we believe will happen will happen. We must train our thoughts to concentrate and focus on the best outcomes and scenarios regardless of what we are experiencing. Oftentimes, we think about the experience we are in more than the solutions necessary to change the experience.

We spend more energy accepting and living in our bad situations than we do seeking answers. Our circumstances don't own us and they can't contain us. We can change the direction of our lives in an instant by just changing our perception. Asking the right questions will help us see things from a completely different perspective immediately.

What can I do with what I have right now to change or improve this situation? How will this affect me if I do nothing? What other alternatives are available to me? Such questions will trigger your subconscious mind to seek solutions and help eliminate fear. Uncontrolled emotions hinder the creative process and doesn't allow ideas to flow freely. This is why some have trouble finding simple solutions to seemingly basic problems. We are capable of solving any problem as long as we know who we are.

No matter what situation we find ourselves in, we can choose to change it by changing our thoughts. How many of you have heard the saying that you are what you eat? The same holds true with your thoughts. You are what you think about all the day long. Look at it this way: We think a thought over and over and over. It eventually becomes a belief. This belief has now entered deep down into your heart. Now you begin to speak what you believe.

Once those two coincide with one another, you will bring into your life everything you speak, good or bad. Since the law of attraction attracts like thoughts, like feelings and like words, everything that you think, say and do will be magnified. The greater it becomes in your life, the more difficult it is to change it.

This is why some struggle with paradigm shifts. The negative things that they have been saying and feeling, they have been saying and feeling for a very long time, and however long that's been, whether months, years or decades, they have attracted a deluge of like thoughts and feelings. At this point, it will take a huge amount of effort to restructure their thinking.

Putting in a lot of effort does not mean that it is impossible. It does mean that you will need to have a strong desire and a no-quit attitude to change from who you are to who you want to be. Everything starts with what you think about who you are. In order for your thoughts to change, your words must be much different than what they have been. The best way to get rid of toxic thinking is to replace the old thoughts with new ones.

Learning to speak positive thoughts will take extreme discipline and a new vision of the life that you want to have. Start small, and then work your way up until you feel the change happening.

How will you know that change is occurring? You will start to feel better about your life and how things are going. Your attitude will begin to change. You will be more joyful and a lot less stressful. You will start making better decisions, and you will begin to feel a shift in your viewpoints and perceptions.

Order will be restored, and shortages and deprivation will begin to dissipate. You'll notice things just begin to work out and your finances become more stable. After a while, you will begin seeing a surplus in all areas of your life. You will start attracting different associates. You will start to build better relationships and develop key connections. Once you begin to realize the control that you have over your life, your level of enthusiasm will elevate. Many of your old acquaintances will attempt to keep you at a level that they feel comfortable with, but don't get pulled into feeling guilty or disloyal. As you transform, old relationships will drop off and new ones will be formed. There will be a battle for control of your thoughts, your time and energy.

Others will be eager to drag you back down to their level so that the guilt of their lack of desire to change doesn't make them feel uncomfortable in your presence. They will offer limitless opinions, rules you should live by and suggestions on what you should do and how you should live. They will remind you of where you came from with no clue as to where you are going. Now that your desires are not in alignment with theirs, they feel inadequately equipped to offer advice. They no longer carry any influence over your decisions, and you feel no desire to respond to their reactions about how to live your life.

Those who you used to be close to will start having difficulty understanding why they are slowly losing you. Subconsciously, they don't want you to move forward or advance in life, because in order to maintain a connection with you, they have to move up to your level or lose the friendship.

For them, keeping you bound to the life that they are accustomed to is much easier than deciding to go after their own dreams. They are not ready to exert the effort or the necessary sacrifices to go where you are going. Seasons change. One season is over as the next season takes hold. Relationships are no different. Some are meant for a season, and others are meant for a lifetime.

Sometimes distinguishing between the two is challenging. The emotions that come with disconnecting from what has become familiar is challenging but necessary if you are to transition from where you are to where you want to be.

Developing new relationships can be risky, scary and uncertain, but they can also be very rewarding. Any time we venture off into the unknown, we are not sure what the future will hold. Until we work up the courage to venture off into the unfamiliar, we will always remain in our comfort zones. As long as we remain living in what's comfortable, we'll never stretch ourselves to live the lives we have imagined.

We all have the capabilities to do the impossible as long as we believe that it is possible. If we want to achieve anything of great significance, we must grasp the power of baby steps. Whether you crawl, walk or run, it is not the pace that determines whether you succeed; it is the ability to continue to move forward. In the game of football, sometimes the hardest yardage to gain is that one single yard. Small things allow you to achieve huge results. Dissect the big picture into small bite-sized pieces, and you'll be amazed at the progress that you will make over time. Doing this affords a couple of things. First, it gives you a very clear and direct path to where you are going. Secondly, it doesn't make it seem so overwhelming and puts a picture in your mind that it is doable.

It is imperative that you always strive to win rather than accept losing. A winning attitude initiates creativity and searches for solutions, whereas a losing attitude finds ways to derail and sabotage your hopes and dreams.

Winning and losing are both created by what we consistently think, say and do. Listen to yourself, and determine what your primary conversations are. The most critical conversations are the ones that we have with ourselves. We talk to ourselves much more than we realize.

Everything we say, whether it is silently or verbally, will either change or maintain the current situation. I would venture to say that, since everything around us is always evolving, flowing with change is probably more natural. Maintaining something takes effort, while giving in to change is effortless.

In summary, dying to self is an ongoing metamorphosis of internal examination and outward transition for moving towards the person that you want to become. Becoming what you have imagined is the ultimate attainment. In your becoming, old beliefs and innate conditioning will slowly be stripped away. Don't fear losing who you were to transition into who you want to become.

Looking back as you are transitioning is only fear working to keep you in a place of bondage to the old you. Don't let the old you win. Recognize that you have decided to grow into your destiny, and boldly continue moving forward knowing that something much better awaits.

Becoming means that you are committing to facing the unknown, because the very thing that you are becoming, you have never been. You don't know the final outcome until you transition to that final stage of becoming. Making room for a better life has conditions, and the prerequisite is that you must die to succeed.

REFERENCES

Neurons to Neighborhoods: The Science of Early Childhood Development, Jack P. Shonkoff and Deborah A. Phillips

The Twelve Universal Laws of Success, Second Edition Expanded, Herbert Harris

The 15 Invaluable Laws of Growth, John C. Maxwell

Think and Grow Rich, Napoleon Hill

The Science of the Mind, Ernest Holmes

The Law of Confession, Dr. Bill Winston

Your Best Life Now, Joel Osteen

The Motivation Manifesto, Brendon Burchard

Beyond the Power of the Subconscious Mind, C. James Jensen

The Richest Man in Babylon, George S. Clason

Day by Day with James Allen, Vic Johnson

The Science of Getting Rich, Wallace D. Wattles

The Master Key System, Charles F. Haanel

The Magic of Thinking Big, Dr. David Schwartz

Unlimited Power, Anthony Robbins

Transform Your Thinking, Transform Your Life, Dr. Bill Winston

Who Moved My Cheese? Dr. Spencer Johnson

Rediscovering the Kingdom, Myles Munroe

As a Man Thinketh, James Allen

The Genie Within: Your Subconscious Mind, Harry W. Carpenter

Atomic Habits, James Clear

Your Invisible Power, Genevieve Behrend

King James Bible, G.E.M. Publishing